CAMBRIDGE LIBRARY COLLECTION

Books of enduring scholarly value

History

The books reissued in this series include accounts of historical events and movements by eye-witnesses and contemporaries, as well as landmark studies that assembled significant source materials or developed new historiographical methods. The series includes work in social, political and military history on a wide range of periods and regions, giving modern scholars ready access to influential publications of the past.

The Seaman's Medical Advocate

Written by a naval surgeon in 1798, this medical treatise provides a frank and harrowing account of life in the British navy. Elliot Arthy started his career as a surgeon's mate in the Africa and West Indies merchant service. He eventually became a surgeon, and worked on a slave ship for many years. In this publication he shows that at least 5,000 seamen were lost to Britain annually through yellow fever and other illnesses, a loss the nation could little afford during wartime. Stressing the 'absolute necessity' for naval surgeons, Arthy's treatise is divided into six parts: the first examines the nature and causes of yellow fever; the second discusses how seamen come into contact with the disease; the third focuses on other causes of the loss of seamen on board ships of war; the fourth on statistics. The fifth and sixth parts suggest methods of prevention.

Cambridge University Press has long been a pioneer in the reissuing of out-of-print titles from its own backlist, producing digital reprints of books that are still sought after by scholars and students but could not be reprinted economically using traditional technology. The Cambridge Library Collection extends this activity to a wider range of books which are still of importance to researchers and professionals, either for the source material they contain, or as landmarks in the history of their academic discipline.

Drawing from the world-renowned collections in the Cambridge University Library, and guided by the advice of experts in each subject area, Cambridge University Press is using state-of-the-art scanning machines in its own Printing House to capture the content of each book selected for inclusion. The files are processed to give a consistently clear, crisp image, and the books finished to the high quality standard for which the Press is recognised around the world. The latest print-on-demand technology ensures that the books will remain available indefinitely, and that orders for single or multiple copies can quickly be supplied.

The Cambridge Library Collection will bring back to life books of enduring scholarly value (including out-of-copyright works originally issued by other publishers) across a wide range of disciplines in the humanities and social sciences and in science and technology.

The Seaman's Medical Advocate

Or, an Attempt to Shew that Five Thousand Seamen are, Annually, During War, Lost to the British Nation through the Yellow Fever

Elliot Arthy

CAMBRIDGE UNIVERSITY PRESS

Cambridge, New York, Melbourne, Madrid, Cape Town,
Singapore, São Paolo, Delhi, Tokyo, Mexico City

Published in the United States of America by Cambridge University Press, New York

www.cambridge.org
Information on this title: www.cambridge.org/9781108028974

This edition first published 1798
This digitally printed version 2011

ISBN 978-1-108-02897-4 Paperback

This book reproduces the text of the original edition. The content and language reflect the beliefs, practices and terminology of their time, and have not been updated.

THE

SEAMAN's

Medical Advocate, &c.

THE

Seaman's Medical Advocate:

OR,

An Attempt to ſhew that FIVE THOUSAND SEAMEN ARE, annually, during War, LOST TO THE BRITISH NATION, in the Weſt-India Merchants' Service, and on-board Ships of War on the Weſt-India Station,

THROUGH THE

YELLOW FEVER,

And other Diſeaſes and Means, from Cauſes which, it is conceived, are chiefly to be obviated, and unconnected with the Misfortunes of War or Dangers of the Seas.

ILLUSTRATED BY CASES AND FACTS.

Moſt reſpectfully ſubmitted to the Conſideration of
The Britiſh Senate;
The Right Honorable the Lords Commiſſioners of the Admiralty;
The Admirals of Fleets, and the Commanders of Ships of War, on the Weſt-India Station;
The Weſt-India Merchants;
And the Commanders of Weſt-India Merchantmen.

By ELLIOT ARTHY, Surgeon,
In the African and Weſt-India Merchants' Service.

LONDON:
Printed for Meſſrs RICHARDSON, Royal-Exchange; and
Mr. EGERTON, oppoſite the Admiralty.
1798.

To the Right Hon. Earl SPENCER,
First Lord of the Admiralty.

MY LORD,

I beg permiſſion to inſcribe this Eſſay to you, not doubting, from your known attention to every thing that regards the welfare of ſeamen and the perfection of the Britiſh navy, but you will give it ſuch patronage as it may appear to merit.

I have the honor to be your Lordſhip's

Moſt reſpectful and

Obedient Servant,

ELLIOT ARTHY.

INTRODUCTION.

TO a nation like Great-Britain dependent on the number, the goodnefs, and the valour, of her feamen, for her protection from foreign enemies, and whofe commerce extends into almoft every known part of the world, the increafe and the prefervation of her feamen muft be, at all times, very highly defirable and neceffary; but now that the nation is engaged in war with all the greateft maritime powers of Europe, and actually threatened with an invafion, they become, I conceive, objects of immediate and moft ferious concern to every honeft Englifhman.

A treatife on a fubject of fuch vaft importance as the prefervation of the health and lives of Britifh mariners, might, perhaps, at this very critical period, with little impropriety, be prefented to the public, without either apology or preface, but, having already employed the pens of fome very eminent phyficians, this additional work may, probably, be deemed unneceffary and, perhaps, even impertinent, more efpecially as coming from the hands of a perfon of little rank in the profeffion.

These circumftances, I conceive, make it requifite for me to trouble the reader with a particular account and explanation of the nature of my work, and of its effential differences from thofe which have been written on the like fubject by other perfons, alfo, of my reafons and qualifications for the undertaking.

At an early period of life, my inclinations led me into the royal navy, wherein I ſerved as a ſurgeon's mate, on the Weſt-India ſtation, for nearly the three laſt years of the American war. During the laſt eight years, I have been employed as a ſurgeon in the African ſlave-trade; at this diſcloſure, I hope the reader will neither be ſhocked nor prejudiced againſt either me or my performance, nor imagine that ſuch a traffic is congenial to my ſentiments, but rather regard my engaging therein as proceeding from the ſecret inſtinct of providence, in order to hereafter anſwer ſome good purpoſe to mankind.

In the courſe of my ſervitude in the royal navy, and in the African ſlave-trade, I have been led to viſit, and make ſome ſtay at, nearly all the Britiſh Weſt-India iſlands, and many hundreds of ſick and hurt ſeamen have come under my inſpection and care; whereby,

I truſt, I ſhall be allowed, at leaſt, to have had ample opportunity of making myſelf acquainted with the nature, the cauſes, and the proper treatment, of diſeaſes incident to ſeamen in the Weſt-Indies, but, above all, with that moſt terrible of plagues, the Yellow Fever.

ARRIVING home juſt at the opening of the medical ſchools, in Autumn, 1796, I thought it my duty to apply a part of the fruits of my labour towards obtaining ſome farther knowledge of my profeſſion, and I accordingly entered myſelf a pupil at the London-Hoſpital. On one of the days, in the month of February following, appropriate to receiving afflicted objects into that charitable houſe, the poor diſabled ſeaman, whoſe caſe is ſtated page 107, preſented himſelf for relief.

HERE let me intreat the reader to turn over and peruſe the caſe I have adverted to, and then figure in his imagination a remarkably fine Britiſh ſeaman, in the very prime of life, utterly diſabled from ſerving his country and gaining ſubſiſtence, through the want of that help from the healing art which happily even the meaneſt individual who toils on-ſhore, for the benefit of either private perſons or the public, now receives, in the moſt ample manner, through the humane, the benevolent, and the philanthropic, ſpirit of the nation.

Let me, alſo, intreat the reader to reflect on the manifold ſervices that Britiſh ſeamen have rendered to their country, and on the almoſt ineſtimable value that each individual of them is at this time of, to the ſtate at large, then will he ſurely greatly regret and be concerned when he is farther intreated to reflect, or, if unacquainted, when I aſſure him that, notwithſtanding the almoſt numberleſs means which Britiſh humanity and benevolence have deviſed and inſtituted, for the relief of human woe, there are yet many thouſands of thoſe moſt uſeful and deſerving people, neceſſitated to croſs the boiſterous main, and to viſit climes dreadfully deſtructive to health and life, in merchant-ſhips not having ſurgeons on-board: the ſad inſtance of the conſequence of it may juſtly enough, I preſume, be ſaid ſuch a glaring overſight of humanity, which I have preſented to his imagination, and it is truſted national policy and benevolence will make him anxious for the redreſs of ſo vaſt an evil.

Such were the feelings and ſentiments of the ſurgeon, to whom the ſeaman related his truly pitiable caſe, and he was thereby involuntarily led at the moment to declare, with a ſpirit truly humane, benevolent, and patriotic, an intention to exert himſelf and his intereſt to the utmoſt, to cauſe the benefits of the healing art to become diſpenſed among ſeamen in the Weſt-India merchants' ſervice.

The lamentable ſituation of the poor fellow made ſo great an impreſſion upon my mind, alſo, that I was irreſtibly led to take up my pen, and commit his caſe to paper, and to make a few deſultory obſervations on the neceſſity for ſurgeons being appointed to Weſt-India merchantmen; intending them for the inſpection of my preceptor, and hoping they might aid him in his benevolent intention.

Having proceeded but a very little way in the buſineſs, my mind became ſo crouded and oppreſſed, with the recollection of the manifold loſs and ſufferings of ſeamen, in both the Weſt-India merchants' ſervice, and on-board ſhips of war on the Weſt-India ſtation, from many other cauſes beſides the want of ſurgical and medical help, and which appeared to me to be equally remediable, that I could not reſiſt nor ſatisfy my feelings as a ſeaman, as an Engliſhman, and as a medical man, until I had committed the whole to paper.

CONTRARY to my expectations, my preceptor expreſſed himſelf of opinion, that what I had written was proper to be communicated to the public, and, fearing that the perilous nature of my occupation might prevent me from doing it at a future period, I was, therefore, encouraged and prompted to ſubmit my manuſcript, without delay, to the preſs, in the hope that the contents would prove uſeful to my country and mankind, and in gratitude to thoſe brave ſeamen who have borne me ſafe from the battle, through many a furious gale, and from many a threatening wave.

The outlines of my work are an attempt to ſhew that there exiſts an abſolute neceſſity for ſurgeons being appointed to Weſt-India merchants' ſhips, alſo, the ſources and means of obviating a very conſiderable part of the preſent dreadful loſs of ſeamen by the Yellow Fever, in the Weſt-India merchants' ſervice, and on-board ſhips of war on the Weſt-India ſtation.

The latter, it muſt be acknowledged, have already been pretty fully treated of, by ſome very able perſons, but, unfortunately, they have generally done it in their medical works, which are chiefly adapted for the peruſal, uſe, and direction, of naval ſurgeons; hence, the legiſlature, and thoſe who have the direction of and command over ſeamen, and on whom the prevention of ſickneſs and accidents chiefly depend, have not been ſo generally nor ſo extenſively aided in their humane endeavours to preſerve the health and lives of ſeamen, as they otherwiſe might have been.

I am, therefore, encouraged to hope that my endeavours to ſhew the means of preſerving, as much as may be, the health and lives of ſeamen, by means independently of medical aid, and in a ſtile calculated for general peruſal, will prove deſerving the attention of the Britiſh ſenate and thoſe right honorable perſonages in whom is veſted the chief direction of our navies, of thoſe, alſo, whom ſeamen more particularly labour to enrich, and of the commanders of both ſhips of war and merchantmen, who muſt oftentimes be greatly diſtreſſed in their minds, and fruſtrated in the execution of the ſervices they are required to perform, by the ſickneſs, diſablement, and loſs, of their ſeamen.

The loud call of humanity, as well as the abſolute neceſſity which I truſt I ſhall ſhew that there really is, for ſurgeons on-board Weſt-India merchant-ſhips, will, I hope, excite that liberality and philanthropy among the Weſt-India merchants and ſhip-owners, for which the Britiſh nation has been ſo long and far famed; and, likewiſe, prove ſome excuſe for my preſuming to treat on the ſubject ſo fully and boldly as I ſhall be found to have done: the advantages which I ſhall alſo point out to accrue to the Weſt-India merchants and ſhip-owners themſelves, as well as to the ſeamen, from the appointment of ſurgeons to their ſhips, and the at preſent very profperous ftate of their branch of commerce, will, I truft, induce and enable them to adopt the feveral regulations I have propofed in their fhips, not only with cheerfulnefs, but, likewife, without the leaft pecuniary inconveniency.

For the fatisfaction of thofe who may deem it neceffary to have higher authority for the truth and fitnefs of the moft material circumftances which I have prefumed to fubmit to public confideration, I fhall refer, as often as occafions require, to Dr. John Hunter's Obfervations on the Difeafes of the Army in Jamaica, from which I with pleafure acknowledge myfelf to have received much affiftance, in both my prefent and paft labours for the relief of afflicted feamen.

I beg leave once more to remark, that the fubfequent treatife was written at intervals of only a few hours leiſure from a courſe of hard ſtudy and ſtrict attendance on an hoſpital, and that, when it was but juſt, in ſuch manner, haſtily committed to paper, I was called upon to go to ſea again, whereby it was deprived of the benefits of a ſecond conſideration, correction, and arrangement, of its parts; theſe unfavorable circumſtances, together with its being my firſt literary eſſay, will, it is hoped, incline the public to receive it with indulgence, and, in ſome degree, apologiſe, for whatever inaccuracies and errors I may be found guilty of: the importance, as well as the humanity, of preſerving, as much as practicable, the health and lives of our ſeamen, will, I alſo hope, warrant the enthuſiaſm with which I have pleaded their cauſe, and, likewiſe, my warmth of expreſſion in deſcribing the human woe I have witneſſed.

SHOULD what is contained in the following ſheets anſwer my ardent wiſh, by proving uſeful to my country and mankind, then will the ſufferings of the helpleſs object, who was the firſt cauſe of their being written, moſt powerfully evince the juſtneſs of the Chriſtian faith, in the exiſtence of an over-ruling providence, that, with infinite wiſdom and goodneſs, ordains many, and for aught we know all, of the afflictions of men, to be productive of ſome future good either to themſelves or to others.

January 15, 1798.

Contents and Arrangement.

THE SIXTH PART. Page 227.

Errors and Omiſſions.

Page 11	Line 17	*For* tornadoes *read* tornado's.
22	—— 6	*Read* for their own recreation.
	—— 15	*For* afflicted by accidents *read* have received accidents.
38	—— 4	*For* he ſent *read* ſent.
39	—— *	*Read* Livid ſpots.
43	—— 2	*For* proſperous, and ſome valuable prizes taken, *read* proſperous; ſome valuable prizes had alſo been taken.
80	—— 17	*For* clearly proved *read* very clearly proved.
96	—— 19	*For* in the ſame way *read* in the ſame manner.
118	—— 5	*For* who have neither authority nor power, *read* who have not ſufficient authority.
123	—— 5	*For* thereto *read* there.
128	—— 18	*For* therein *read* there.
208	—— 3	*For* as they often do. I have *read* as they often do, and I have.

THE FIRST PART.

OF THE NATURE AND CAUSES OF THE BILIOUS OR YELLOW FEVER.

THE loſs of ſeamen, I have aſſerted and undertaken to demonſtrate, being chiefly occaſioned by the Yellow Fever, it may be ſatisfactory to the curious, as well as neceſſary to make myſelf clearly underſtood by ſuch of my readers as have not had a medical education, to commence with an account of the nature and caufes of that moft prevailing and rapacious difeafe.

NATURE, in all warm climates, is moft abundantly prolific in animal and vegetable productions: the furface of the earth abounds with plants, fhrubs, trees, and reptiles; the air and the waters with innumerable infects; all which, through the heat of the fun, moft rapidly fpring into exiftence, arrive at maturity, and fall into decay.

THE heat of the fun, aided by rain, which falls in great abundance at certain times of the year, occafions thofe various animal and vegetable productions, which are conftantly rifing in profufe fucceffion, to putrefy and emit fubtle effluvia, which, through their tenuity and lightneſs, become diffuſed and buoyant in the air; and, being mixed with, or rather enveloped by, the moiſture exhaled by the heat of the ſun, through the day, from the ſurface of the earth, of rivers, and of ſtagnant waters, they riſe into the atmoſphere; and when, after the ſetting of the ſun, theſe humid particles fall to the earth, in the form of dew, thoſe effluvia deſcend therewith, and according to the degree of the heat of the atmoſphere, are either raiſed or depreſſed, and as the wind blows, ſo they are alſo driven to and fro.

I have ſmelt theſe effluvia moſt offenſively during thick fogs, which prevail at the cloſe of the rainy ſeaſon, in Africa, and had them wafted to my ſenſes, by the wind, from the oppoſite ſide of a river more than two miles broad.

THE effluvia ſo generated, from putrid animal and vegetable matter, are particularly baneful and deſtructive to the health and life of mankind; and when they come in contact with the bodies of, or are inhaled by, perſons not nurtured in the Weſt-Indies, and who are, beſides, either juſt arrived in full health and vigour, and, conſequently, unſeaſoned to the climate, or who are weakened by diſeaſe, fatigue, bad living, mental inquietude, hard drinking, or who have laboured much under the mid-day ſun, they occaſion that diſeaſe commonly called in the Weſt-Indies the Bilious and Yellow Fever.

THESE effluvia being nearer to the

ſurface of the earth by night, expoſure under the unfavorable ſtates of conſtitution mentioned, will be more hazardous then than by day, when the warmth of the ſun elevates and diffuſes them in the atmoſphere.

So it happens, that ſeamen, whoſe habits, diſpoſitions, and employments, hereafter to be mentioned, occaſion them to be much, and at all times and ſeaſons, committing intemperances on-ſhore, in the Weſt-Indies, are ſo liable, and ſo frequently fall a ſacrifice, to the Bilious or Yellow Fever.

On the contrary, perſons born and brought up in the Weſt-Indies, and even Europeans, who are of a mean temperament, between glowing and declining health, who take moderate exercise, eat sparingly of good and wholesome food, drink a little wine or spirits daily, are of a cheerful disposition, and who do not expose themselves to the night air, nor to the mid-day sun, are in a favorable condition, and not disposed, to be affected by the poison, which may justly enough be said to be constantly floating in the air of the West-Indies and all other warm climates.

AGAIN, though the sea abounds with myriads and myriads of living creatures, yet there is no such noxious effluvia produced from them, for they all, from the biggest to the least, prey upon each other. The surface of the great deep is, also, continually agitated by the trade-wind, which together with the antiſeptic quality of the ſalt with which it is impregnated, prevents its ſtagnating and becoming putrid; ſo that the potent rays of the ſun exhale nothing, from the immenſely wide and extended main, but a pure watery vavour, which, as well as the great heat of the ſun between the tropics, when alone, and uncombined with the aforeſaid effluvia, is not particularly unfriendly to the human conſtitution. In the open ſea of the Weſt-Indics, therefore, and at ſuch diſtances from the land where the ſaid poiſonous effluvia do not reach, the air is pure and untainted by any noxious matter; hence, while ſhips are at ſea, and even when in harbour, if they are not moored near to unhealthy ſituations, the ſeamen, if kept conſtantly on-board, in a regular and ſober performance of their duty, will. and do in general, enjoy as good health as in any other part of the world: ſo it is, that ſhips conſtantly arrive in the Weſt-Indies, from Europe and other equally high northern, as well as ſouthern, latitudes, with their crews in perfect health, and entirely free from the Yellow Fever; provided, I beg leave to have it underſtood, they have not touched at any port by the way, and thereby been expoſed to the aforeſaid peſtilential effluvia.

In proportion as different countries and iſlands, and as different parts of countries and of iſlands, ſituated between the tropics, abound with wood, with ſtagnant waters, and marſhy tracts of land, favorable to the production of vegetable and animal matter; in proportion, alſo, to the heat of the ſun, and the more or leſs rain, at different periods of the year, favoring or not favoring the putrefaction of ſuch vegetable and animal ſubſtances, and the eſcape therefrom of the aforeſaid peſtilential effluvia; and, according as thoſe effluvia are nearer to, or diſtant from, the ſurface of the earth; ſo is one country or one iſland, one part of a country or of an iſland, one ſeaſon of the year, one part of the day and of the night, more healthy or unhealthy than another.

So that on dry and rather elevated parts, where the land is cleared of wood and in a ſtate of cultivation, and during the dry ſeaſon of the year, there is little or no ſuch poiſon to human life produced. But, in low marſhy ſituations, where the land is overgrown with wood, alſo, in the neighbourhood of large lakes of ſtagnant waters, and on the banks of large rivers which undergo a conſiderable ebb of tide, ſuch parts, in the rainy ſeaſon of the year, are ſcarcely habitable, through the abundance and malignancy of the produced effluvia. Even parts far diſtant, that would otherwiſe be very healthy, feel their influence through the medium of the wind; whereby, it happens, that ſhips moored off ſuch unhealthy ſituations, though at ſome diſtance, yet, when the wind ſets to them from the land, will have their crews, in an otherwiſe unaccountable manner, taken ſick of the Yellow Fever.

THE wind does, alſo, ſometimes, prove the means of reſtoring health in parts; and on the riſing of a violent gale or a hurricane, the Yellow Fever, which was juſt before then raging with the moſt rapacious fury, amongſt the inhabitants of large towns, has ſuddenly abated, and even diſappeared. A remarkable inſtance of it is given in Mr. John Halliday's Account of the Putrid Bilious Fever, which raged in the City of the Havanna, in the Months of June, July, and Part of Auguſt, 1794. And the like often occurs on the coaſt of Africa, where tornadoes prevail, which are ſudden and violent guſts of wind, that blow for a few minutes with fury equal to a Weſt-India hurricane, and are accompanied by a prodigious deal of thunder, lightning, and rain. Theſe ſalutary events are no doubt occaſioned by the immenſe violence of the wind, together with the exceſſive thunder, lightning, and torrents of rain, with which it is commonly accompanied, clearing the atmoſphere of an unuſual quantity of peſtilential effluvia: and make it probable if an hurricane were to happen at this time, that the Weſt-Indies would be thereby rendered leſs unhealthy, and were it not for the horrid devaſtation it would otherwiſe commit, it is, I conceive, an event much to be deſired.

According to the different degrees of virulence in the contagion, at different times, and in different places; according, alſo, as the ſeveral habits, intemperances, and employments, of perſons, produce different degrees of ſuſceptibility to be affected thereby; and, as their conſtitutions, overcome, or yield to, its baneful influence; ſo, have different perſons the Bilious or Yellow Fever, ſooner or later, more frequently and more favorably, more violently and more fatally, than others. Some it attacks ſuddenly and deſtroys even in a few hours; others are not apparently affected for a conſiderable length of time; and, others, have it ſteal upon them inſenſibly, and linger for a long while, before they either recover or fall victims. Thus, it ſometimes obliges ſeamen to leave their work on a ſudden; others, it attacks during the night-watch; others, when on duty in boats; and, others, after they have departed and got many leagues from the Weſt-Indies, and even conſiderably to the northward or ſouthward of the tropics.

THE firſt attack of the Yellow Fever that a European has, after arriving in the Weſt-Indies, is commonly called a ſeaſoning, which, when very violent, though the perſon recover, is not to be regarded as favorable, in as much as it generally impairs his conſtitution ſo much as to render him, during his reſidence in the Weſt-Indies, ſuſceptible of frequent and periodical relapſes, which, at length, ſap his ſtamina ſo much as to leave him little or no enjoyment, nor chance for his life, but by relinquishing his ambitious projects and hopes of amassing a fortune, and returning to Europe.

Some few Europeans, have the seasoning, as it is called, moderate, and their constitutions not being thereby much impaired, they become naturalized to the climate, and, through the exercise of temperance, they enjoy a tolerably good state of health, until by industry they are made affluent: but, where one European, who settles in the West-Indies, is so fortunate, thousands fall an early sacrifice to the Yellow Fever; an awful warning this for British youths to confine their wants, their desires, and their ambition, within the pale of reason and of nature; and not to leave their native ſoil, where freedom, health, and plenty, prevail, for a country that ſo rarely affords other than either a miſerable or precarious exiſtence.

It is worthy of remark, that the Weſt-Indies produce no remedy for the plague with which we may ſay it is infeſted. And, farther, of all the medicines, and medicinal compoſitions, which, by the induſtry of man and the reſearches of the learned, have been extorted from, and diſcovered in, the mineral, the vegetable, and the animal, kingdoms of nature, in this and every other known part of the world, and which are almoſt innumerable, none are ſo generally, nor ſo ſovereignly, efficacious, in counteracting the bad effects of the faid effluvia on the human body, as the Peruvian Bark, which is the produce of a country many thoufand miles diftant, and not to be obtained otherwife than by croffing a vaft ocean, a grand and mighty proof this, that nations as well as individuals were created for each others aid and relief, and not to deftroy one the other by cruel, unprovoked, and ambitious, wars.

In England, many perfons are of opinion that the Yellow Fever is more violent in its nature and effects, in the Weft-Indies, during war than peace, which I conceive to have originated from our having in war time a greater number of troops and fhips of war in the Weft-Indies, and from, perhaps, many additional perfons going there, to tranſact either public or private buſi-neſs, whereby more deaths muſt conſe-quently happen by the Yellow Fever, which, through the medium of newſ-papers, and of private letters and per-ſons, oftener engage the public as well as individuals attention, and, very na-turally, excites a belief that the Yellow Fever is, at ſuch times, unuſually malig-nant, when, in fact, it is only the effect of an additional number being expoſed to its influence. Some years, as well as ſeaſons of the year, in the Weſt-In-dies, are, no doubt, more unhealthy than others, and greater numbers die of the Yellow Fever at one period than another: but ſuch occurrences happen during peace as well as war.

THE terms Bilious and Yellow Fever

are ufed only by the vulgar and unlearned; the former arofe from the bilious vomitings with which fome perfons are affected; and the latter arofe from a fuffufion of bile which occurs in fome perfons, and caufes the whole body, and fometimes the different fecretions therefrom, to appear yellow: fuch bilious vomitings and yellownefs are meer adventitious circumftances, and owing, I conceive, to the different effects of the poifonous effluvia, produced in warm climates, on different conftitutions: fo that, whether there be thofe bilious vomitings, or that yellownefs of the fkin, or not, the difeafe is to be regarded as the fame, as differing, only, in degree, and, as owing to the fame caufes, namely, effluvia from putrid animal and vegetable ſubſtances; and is called, by phyſicians, the Remittent Fever of Tropical Climates; becauſe, it is found to be the grand and univerſally prevailing diſeaſe, within thoſe latitudes, all round the world, as well as in the Weſt-Indies; and becauſe, perſons affected thereby have, at intervals, a remiſſion or abatement of their complaints. In compliance, however, with cuſtom, and that I may be better underſtood, I ſhall not adopt any new term, but call the diſeaſe, produced as I have deſcribed, by its too well known, and often repeated, name, Yellow Fever.

THE SECOND PART.

OF THE SEVERAL HABITS, DISPOSITIONS, AND EMPLOYMENTS, OF SEAMEN, IN THE WEST-INDIA MERCHANTS' SERVICE; WHEREBY, THEY ARE EXPOSED, AND PREDISPOSED, TO BE AFFECTED BY THE YELLOW FEVER. AND, OF THE OTHER ASSERTED DISEASES AND MEANS, WHICH CONTRIBUTE TO THE LOSS OF SEAMEN.

THE former are, frequent deſertion from one ſhip to another, in order to obtain more wages, or, rather, a large ſum of money for the run-home from the Weſt-Indies; leaving their ſhips, and going on-ſhore, to avoid being impreſſed; going in open boats, to diſtant parts, to fetch their ſhip's lading and water; going on-ſhore, with and for their commanders and other officers, by night, and for recreation; and, laſtly, the intemperances they commit when, on thoſe ſeveral occaſions, they are on-ſhore.

THE latter are, want of a proper ſleeping-place, attendance, and medical and ſurgical aſſiſtance, when ſick of the Yellow Fever; when, alſo, they are affected with the venereal diſeaſe, and afflicted by accidents.

SECTION THE FIRST.

Of the production of the Yellow Fever, and consequent loss of seamen, in the West-India merchants' service, through their desertion from one ship to another, in order to obtain more wages, or, rather, a large sum of money for the run-home from the West-Indies; through, also, their leaving their ships, and going on-shore, to avoid being impressed; and through the intemperances they commit, when, on those several occasions, they are on-shore.

THE reader's attention muſt be, in the firſt place, directed to the ſeveral Britiſh merchantmen that are engaged in the Weſt-India trade, both importing ſupplies and carrying away its produce; which amount, in all, to about one thouſand ſail of ſhipping, of, from one to five hundred tons burthen and upwards, and navigated with from ten to thirty, and ſome few forty, and even fifty, men, each: of theſe ſhips, it may be computed, that about three-fourths are what are commonly termed Weſt-India men, or ſugar-ſhips, belonging to the ſeveral ports of England, Scotland, and Ireland: the other fourth may be conſidered as compoſed of African ſlave-ſhips, together with a few veſſels of rather inconſiderable burthen from Newfoundland and North-America.

By theſe ſeveral veſſels, upwards of twenty thouſand ſeamen are annually conveyed to the Weſt-Indies. (Vide Mr. Baillie's ſpeech in the Houſe of Commons, on the abolition of the ſlave-trade, the 2d of April, 1792.) And, it is a very pleaſant fact to reflect upon, that, excepting the African ſlave-ſhips, little or no ſickneſs is ever experienced on the paſſage, ſo that nearly the whole of that vaſt body of ſeamen, almoſt invariably, barring accidents, arrive in a good ſtate of health in the Weſt-Indies: and, what is equally true, would generally remain and return ſo, if there were any means of reſtraining their imprudences, and keeping them on-board their reſpective ſhips, in a regular and ſober performance of their duty: Of all this, I have had an exceſs of evidence, both in the merchants' ſervice and on board our ſhips of war; and the ſame is obſerved by Dr. John Hunter, page 107 of his "Obſervations on the "Diſeaſes of the Army in Jamaica." But unfortunately, from circumſtances which I ſhall next bring to view, a very conſiderable change in their health, and decreaſe of their numbers begin to take place ſoon after their arrival.

The men of war are exceedingly vigilant in the impreſſing of ſeamen in the Weſt-Indies, ſo that, if a merchantman arrive at a port much frequented by men of war, a great part of her crew ſoon falls into their hands, and the reſt, partly to avoid the like misfortune, as they think it is, and partly to obtain what is called a run-home, the nature of which will ſoon be explained, leave the ſhip entirely, to be diſcharged of her cargo and reladen, at a great expence to the owners, by negroes. If a merchantman arrive at a port or iſland only occaſionally viſited by men of war, the ſeamen are preſerved for a long time, and often all eſcape being impreſſed, by going on-ſhore, on the report or appearance of a ſhip of war coming in, and repairing on-board again, when ſhe is gone or the report proving to have been falſe, which occaſions a conſiderable and frequent interruption to the buſineſs of the ſhip. If again, a merchantman arrive at a port ſeldom or never viſited by men of war, the crew are kept on-board, and the buſineſs of the ſhip goes on tolerably well, until near the period when a convoy of men of war is appointed to protect a fleet of merchantmen home. Preciſely the ſame tranſactions take place amongſt the healthy part of the crews of ſlave-ſhips, according as they go to ports more or leſs frequented by men of war.

The whole of theſe ſeamen, it muſt now be obſerved, are engaged, at the commencement of their ſeveral voyages, in Europe and other parts, for from one to four pounds per month wages each, according as they are either boys or landmen, ordinary or able ſeamen: but, as ſoon as they arrive in the Weſt-Indies, ſuch as are ſo fortunate as to eſcape being impreſſed, begin to bend their minds to what is called a good run-home, which is a ſum of money for the bare taſk of working a ſhip from the Weſt-Indies home; and amounts to from ten to fifty, and ſixty, guineas; varying at times and places, according to the plenty or ſcarcity of ſeamen, and the greater or leſs number of ſhips requiring men. Such, I am told, was the demand for ſeamen, at Jamaica, on the ſailing of the July Fleet, in 1796, that even ſeventy guineas were given to ſeamen for the run-home.

The giving ſuch a great ſum of money for ſo ſhort a ſervice, is one of the chief ſources of the loſs of ſeamen I have advanced and am now about to prove: it in the firſt place, occaſions many to deſert from the ſhips of war, and thoſe again, in the merchants' ſervice, remain no longer ſatisfied, on-board their reſpective ſhips, than till they hear of a ſhip or ſhips wanting runners, as they are called. So that from the different ſources of ſeamen deſerting from the ſhips of war, and thoſe deſerting from the merchantmen, ſome to avoid being impreſſed, and all having one common object in view, namely, that of getting a good run-home, it happens that there is, almoſt conſtantly, a vaſt number of ſeamen on-ſhore throughout the Weſt-Indies, particularly as the time draws nigh for the ſailing of a large fleet of merchantmen, under the protection of men of war, when the ſeamen know the largeſt runs will be given. The conſequence is, that, in order to ſcreen themſelves from being impreſſed, and to get to diſtant parts of iſlands for the benefit of larger runs, they are obliged to lurk about the outſkirts of towns, and to travel on foot a long way through the country; very often, obliged to take up their lodging by the road ſide, or in a cane-patch, expoſed to the peſtilential influence of the night-air, to rain, and to the intenſe heat of the ſun by day; ſometimes faſting, at others intoxicated, for ſeveral hours, and even days, together.

THE nature of ſuch irregularities and of the climate,* it will now be clearly

* See Dr. Hunter's Obſervations, Pages 108 and 109.

underſtood, makes it next to a miracle if any of them eſcape the Yellow Fever: and they really are, almoſt all, ſooner or later, affected thereby; ſome only a few hours after landing, others when got to a diſtance from any town, and others not till they are got out to ſea again; and what is ſtill farther to be lamented, from either not having any money, nor any claim on any one for aſſiſtance, or being at ſea in a ſhip not having a ſurgeon on-board, many of them have to ſtruggle through, and others die of, their diſeaſes, without medical aſſiſtance, and ſometimes I am afraid without even the neceſſary food for the ſupport and reſtoration of nature.

I ſhall, in the next place, endeavour

to prove and elucidate these said general assertions, opinions, and principles, by

CASES AND FACTS.

FIRST. — The Sl--p Sw--t, W-----m B-lt-n commander, of Bristol, of which vessel I was surgeon, arrived in the harbour of St. John's, Antigua, in the month of October, 1793, after a slaving-voyage, with a crew consisting of twenty men and boys, all in perfectly good health, and three-fourths of them were remarkably good, able, and fine high-spirited, seamen.

A ship of war coming in, soon after our arrival, those fine fellows all went on shore, and the c-pt--n sent them, with a note, to the manager of a neighbouring plantation, begging they might have ſhelter thereon, until the ſhip of war was gone. The manager immediately diſmiſſed them back to our captain, with a note, ſaying, he had met with ſo much ingratitude from ſailors, and they had committed ſo many depredations on the eſtate, even when under its protection from the preſs, that he was determined never to ſcreen any more of them: this reply, I recollect, very much irritated our captain, who, being of a high martial ſpirit, debated a long time within himſelf, whether or not the inſult of refuſing protection to his men was not deſerving of a challenge; at length, however, cool reaſon and peace prevailed, and he told the men to make the beſt ſhift they could, for their preſervation from the preſs, for the preſent, and he would provide them a place of ſecurity therefrom, againſt a future time: the poor fellows obeyed, and the recital of the conſequences muſt, I am ſure, agitate the feelings of every lover of his country, and of every perſon that has the leaſt regard or ſympathy for the ſufferings of its brave defenders.

THEY went, after the manner I have deſcribed, a conſiderable way out of town, and not being able to obtain any ſettled ſhelter, were expoſed in open fields, by night and day, for ſome time, drinking, I am afraid, very hard, and getting but little ſuſtenance, till, in a few days, word was ſent on-board to me, from the captain, one morning very early, defiring me to go on-fhore immediately, and fee the cooper, who was taken very bad in the country.

Knowing the inftantaneous and dangerous manner in which the Yellow Fever fometimes makes its attack, I immediately went on-fhore, but juft before I landed, a fecond meffenger had been fent to acquaint the captain that the cooper was dead; and but too true it was! for, in two or three hours after, his corpfe was brought into town by his comrades, who were now fo much fatigued with what they had undergone, and fo greatly difpirited by the fudden lofs of the cooper, that they determined to run all rifk of being impreffed, rather than fly into the country for refuge any more.

THE cooper, by the reft of our peoples account, had complained of a flight pain in his head, and of being otherwife rather poorly, for two or three days before his deceafe, but his complaints did not become any way ferious until the evening before he died, when, to ufe their own words, "neither grog "nor kind language would cheer him, "and he began to talk about dying, "which very much alarmed them, and "the next morning they fet about con-"veying him to town, but, before they "had proceeded far, he died by the "road fide."

The manager of the eftate, on which the cooper died, being informed of the circumſtance by ſome of his negroes, and impreſſed, by the ſuddenneſs of his death, with an idea that it was occaſioned by maltreatment, he ſent a note to that purport to the coroner, who ſummoned a jury, in conſequence, to inveſtigate the truth; when, there not appearing to be any marks of violence done to the body, and his comrades repeating the above account, of his complaints and death, in a very clear as well as pathetic manner, the coroner and jury being alſo told of his previous expoſure to the cauſes of the Yellow Fever, and knowing well the ſudden manner in which that diſeaſe often terminates life, their verdict was, that he died by the viſitation of God.

A day or two after interring the

cooper, one of the ſeamen was ſent on-board to me in the laſt ſtage of the Yellow Fever, being in a ſtate of low delirium, and his body covered with petechiæ,* and, notwithſtanding my utmoſt endeavours, he died on the ſecond day after.

About the ſame time, another of the ſeamen, who left us as ſoon as the cooper was buried, was attacked with the Yellow Fever, while on the road to join a privateer, lying in a neighbouring harbour, and carried off in a very few hours.

The carpenter, and another ſeaman, fell into the hands of a preſs-gang, who, conſequently, took them on-board a

* Spots denoting imminent danger.

ſhip of war, wherein they, alſo, were ſhortly after ſeized by the Yellow Fever, which ended their days.

FIVE others had, alſo, very ſevere attacks of the Yellow Fever, from which I had very great difficulty in recovering them.

THE other half of our crew ran away and got out to ſea, and to a ſober regular conduct in other veſſels, which probably preſerved their lives.

THUS, the country loſt two excellent mechanics, a carpenter and a cooper, and three fine ſeamen; and our crew was reduced to a few invalids; all within about a fortnight.

SECOND.—The Sl--p Sw--t, and myſelf in her, tarried a whole year at Antigua, and as often as a ſhip of war came in, we were under the neceſſity of ſending the few people we had to ſecrete themſelves on-ſhore, which was almoſt uniformly followed by ſickneſs, though happily no more deaths happened. I was often myſelf ſubjected to the midnight inſults of preſs-gangs, and obliged to fly into the country for refuge, which occaſioned me more ſickneſs than ever I experienced, even on the deadly coaſt of Africa. In my flights and excurſions, I often ſaw ſeamen labouring under the moſt violent attacks of the Yellow Fever, entirely dependent on, and conſigned to the management of, indigent negro women, and ſorry I am to ſay, one of them, who had nurſed ſome of our ſick people, and who had watched them, with the moſt affectionate and unremitted care and attention, night and day, as well as provided them with ſuſtenance, and ſuch other little neceſſaries and comforts as ſick perſons require, until they were quite reſtored to health, was left incumbered with a debt, incurred for the ſame, requiring, in her little ways and means, a long ſeries of induſtry to diſcharge. The ſeaman's generoſity is ſo well known, that it is almoſt needleſs for me to ſay, they would have paid her had it been in their power, and, as it was not, they could only refer her to thoſe who were indebted to them for their ſervices, and whoſe negligence in ſo doing was the more unpardonable, and to be wondered at, as the voyage had to that period been exceedingly profperous, and fome valuable prizes taken in the courfe thereof: the feamen, in confequence, on their recovery, left the fervice of a mafter who had treated them, I may fay, fo outrageoufly unjuftly and illiberally. I have, purpofely, been full and particular on this circumftance, as I fhall have occafion to advert to it hereafter.

PRECISELY the fame tranfactions were going on, on-board of the other merchantmen, as often as a fhip of war vifited the place; fo that almoft every day brought accounts to me of feamen taken fick of the Yellow Fever, in confequence of their going on-fhore to avoid being impreffed; which occafioned, as may be judged, many deaths within the twelve months of my continuance at Antigua.

THIRD.—Through the aforesaid sickness, deaths, desertion, and impressing, of our people, it happened, that, when the Sl--p Sw--t left Antigua, she had nearly a fresh crew of twenty hands, and all of them were, fortunately, in a perfectly good state of health.

The day after sailing, the vessel unfortunately sprung a dangerous leak, which obliged us to put into St. K-t's, to have it stopped; and there, again, commenced the business of going onshore, occasionally, to avoid being impressed, which caused, as it always does, several of the crew to be attacked with the Yellow Fever, and in little better than a week, the veſſel became, once more, like an hoſpital, having only ten ſick people belonging to her; all the reſt having either been impreſſed, or ran away in ſearch of a larger ſum for the run-home to England.

FORTUNATELY, none of the ſick, at this time, died, but the ungrateful fellows, as they got well, deſerted, like the reſt, for the ſake of getting more money for the run-home; ſo that a third crew was obliged to be engaged, to navigate the veſſel from the Weſt-Indies.

FOURTH. — The Sh-p P-lg--m, of B--t--l, Captain M-nt-r, of which ſhip, I was, alſo, ſurgeon, arrived in the month of March, 1796, at Kingſton, Jamaica, after a ſlaving voyage, with a crew of thirty-five men, all in perfect health. Here, fortunately for the health and lives of the people, the vigilance of the impreſs officers was ſuch, that two-thirds of them fell into their hands, within a week after the ſhip's arrival, and, conſequently, before many of them had been at all on-ſhore, by which they eſcaped the Yellow Fever.

Some of the others, alſo, eſcaped the Yellow Fever, by leaving us entirely, and engaging themſelves in other merchantmen, and ſailing from the Weſt-Indies, without being much expoſed on-ſhore.

Two, however, of this crew, who eſcaped the vigilance of the preſs, and in evading them were much expoſed, as well as guilty of great intemperances, on-ſhore, had very violent attacks of the Yellow Fever, which very nearly terminated their exiſtence.

SINCE my return to England, I have had the pleaſure of hearing of the ſafe return and welfare of nearly the whole of the reſt of the crew, who were impreſſed, and deſerted from us, at Jamaica, which I am firmly and clearly of opinion, would not have been their good fortune, had they continued but a little while longer at hide and ſeek on-ſhore, in the Weſt-Indies.

FIFTH.—The laſt-mentioned Ship, to wit, the P-lg--m, after the ſale of her cargo at Kingſton, went down to S-v-n-a la Marr, and in company with ſeveral other Weſt-India men, loaded with Weſt-Indian produce, and departed with the very next convoy, in the month of June following.

The general rendezvous of the fleet, Bluefields, previous to our final departure from the Weſt-Indies, is very little diſtant from Savanna la Marr, on which account, as the time for ſailing drew nigh, the harbour became reſorted to by ſeamen from ſundry other, and very diſtant, parts of the iſland, in order to ſhip themſelves by the run-home.

Some of theſe ſeamen, conceiving that there would not be much run-money given in the place, betook themſelves to other ports, in hopes of getting more; while, others, conceiving that times would mend, or, probably, not having money to ſupport them any longer, nor to carry them farther, ſtayed and hired themſelves to work on-board the ſhipping, until the departure of the convoy.

FOUR were engaged, at different times, on-board the P-lg--m, in order to get her in readineſs for ſea: they had all deſerted from ſhips at a conſiderable diſtance, and had travelled through the country on-foot, expoſed very often to the mid-day ſun; frequently taking up their lodging by the road ſide, without any ſhelter from the night air; often faſting for a conſiderable time, and, as may naturally be ſuppoſed, to the utmoſt of their finances, indulging themſelves in the uſe of ſtrong drinks.

ONE of them came on-board, quite exhauſted with fatigue and hunger, inſomuch, that, at firſt, he requeſted only a belly full of victuals for his ſervices; but, as ſoon as he had regained his ſtrength and vigour, he aſked a very extravagant ſum of money, which was granted him, in order to retain him in the ſhip: as ſoon, however, as he heard that more wages, and a larger ſum of money for the run-home, was given in other ſhips, he left us; and ſo he went, out of one ſhip into another, two or three times, till, in a few days, after leaving us, he was arreſted by the Yellow Fever and died.

A ſecond left us for the ſame reaſon,

becaufe he was affured of a larger run on-board of another fhip: this man, when he came on-board, had feveral venereal ulcers and two buboes, on which account, he was very much eafed from duty; but, neither his prefent eafe, nor the opportunity of obtaining a cure, through my care, were fufficient to retain him in the fhip; and he went, in the ftate I have defcribed, on-board of another not having a furgeon, which fhip not ftaying long enough in the Weft-Indies, for him to obtain a radical cure, by the hands of any medical man on-fhore, it is likely that his conftitution, if not his life, fuffered, in the end, through his ingratitude and inconfiderate nefs.

A third of thefe men left us on a very

trifling pretext, no doubt with the ſame mercenary views as the other two, and going on-ſhore, was, in two or three days after, attacked with the Yellow Fever, from which he had a moſt miraculous eſcape with life, not having any money, nor the leaſt claim on any one for aſſiſtance, during his ſickneſs.

THE fourth, and laſt, who was as fine a ſeaman as ever ſerved his country, after having wrought moſt manfully on-board of us, for about a week, was taken with the Yellow Fever, which, notwithſtanding my utmoſt endeavours, carried him off within eight and forty hours.

SECTION THE SECOND.

Of the production of the Yellow Fever, and consequent loss of seamen, in the West-India merchants' service, through their going in open boats, to distant parts, to fetch their ships' lading and water; through going on-shore with and for their commanders and other officers at night, and for their own recreation; through, also, the intemperances they commit, when, on those several occasions, they are on-shore; and, lastly, their loss and sufferings through want of a proper sleeping-place, attendance, and medical assistance, when sick of the Yellow Fever.

THE Ship P-Jg--m's going, as mentioned in the laſt ſection, to Savanna la Marr, to load with Weſt-Indian produce, gave me a farther opportunity of witneſſing the unſalutary and fatal conſequences of ſeamen's wandering about, and committing intemperances, onſhore, in the Weſt-Indies; and of obſerving the ſeveral cauſes of ſickneſs and death, through the Yellow Fever, which ſeamen are liable and expoſed to, in the courſe of the buſineſs of loading a Weſt-Indiaman, in peace as well as war, the recital of which will form the preſent ſection.

WE preſerved ſeven of our original crew from being impreſſed and from deſertion at Kingſton; and Savanna la

Marr being an out-port, very rarely vifited by men of war, the bufinefs of loading the P-lg--m went on, the whole time, without any interruption from fhips of war, after the manner that it ufually does, in the regular Weft-India-men, during peace.

OUR people were fent in boats, to diftant parts, to collect the cargo and to fetch water, in which fervices they were often expofed many hours, and even whole nights, and during all weathers, either in the open boat or on-fhore, without any fhelter.

THEY frequently went, likewife, after labouring hard, and fweating profufely, through the day, to take the captain to and from the fhore by night, and, on fuch occafions, were not unfrequently obliged to wait his conveniency until very late hours, and ſometimes even till day-light, during which, overcome as they were by previous fatigue, and not being able to keep themſelves awake, they laid down in the boat and ſlept in the open air, and that often during the falling of very heavy dews.

THEY, alſo, ſometimes went on-ſhore, for their own recreation, and, at times, ſtaid late.

ALMOST as often as they went on-ſhore, on any of the above occaſions, if they had no money, ſome part or other of their wearing apparel was taken, to be bartered away for new rum, ſo that they were frequently in a ſtate of intoxication, when expoſed to thoſe inclemencies of the weather and ſure uſherers of the Yellow Fever.

After a very few trips on-ſhore, the whole of them were moſt violently attacked with the Yellow Fever.

The Ship, at the time of their being taken ſick, was ſo far laden, and the decks, both above and below, were ſo lumbered with the cargo and ſtores of various kinds, that there was neither ſhelter nor ſleeping-place for them beneath any of the decks, nor ſcarcely room to ſpread a bed any where above deck: the quarter-deck, which was equally lumbered, had a ſlight canvas awning over it, which afforded a partial ſcreen from the night-air, from rain, and from the ſcorching ſun, under which the poor fellows laid down, wherever they could find a ſpacé of their length and breadth. Moſt of them were without beds, and had ſold nearly all their clothes, ſo that they were obliged to lie on the bare planks, and in the ſame dirty clothes, from their attack to near their recovery. An old ſail was, after ſome time, obtained, to eaſe their fretted limbs from the painful hardneſs of the deck, and to cover them by night, which is to be conſidered as a great and rare indulgence, at leaſt as far as my obſervation has extended.

Such, moreover, was the eagerneſs and hurry to get the ſhip loaded, that no one could be ſpared to attend upon the ſick, though ſeveral negroes were employed on-board at the time; ſo that if I had not been on-board, or ſome one elſe in my ſtation, who could not with propriety have been put to other duty beſides attending them and adminiſtering their medicines, the greater part of them muſt, I am confident, have died through meer neglect: for their complaints were truly ſo violent, and ſo greatly aggravated by the many inconveniences and inclemencies of the weather they had to contend with, that I found it a taſk of no ſmall difficulty to reſtore them to health, with even the moſt aſſiduous attention to them, night and day, and, I may ſay, a long experience of their complaints and conſtitutions.

THE foregoing circumſtances may be conſidered as ſpecimens of what muſt be often occurring among ſeamen in the loading of Weſt-Indiamen, with theſe conſiderable aggravations, that thoſe ſhips having generally no ſurgeon, nor any one elſe, whoſe peculiar duty is to attend the ſeamen when ſick, they muſt, and do I am ſure, ſuffer very much, and even die, for want of proper attendance, and ſupply of victuals and drink, as well as medicines: I had, in truth, the moſt abundant proofs of it among the Weſt-Indiamen that were loading in company with us, as I ſhall in the next place ſhew.

THERE were two ſurgeons in the vicinity of the harbour, but one of them was of very indifferent repute, and the other would not go on ſhip board, except on very particular occaſions, ſuch as, I ſuppoſe, to viſit a captain, or other perſon, who would pay him largely; on which accounts, I was frequently ſent for, to viſit the ſick ſeamen of other ſhips: their complaints invariably proved to be the Yellow Fever, in a greater or leſs degree, and manifeſtly traceable from their having been expoſed on their ſhips duty, or otherwiſe, whole nights, and in all weathers, either in open boats or on-ſhore, and rambling about drinking hard. I, alſo, often found that they had been two or three days ſick before I was ſent for, and had no proper place to repoſe in; and, although, on my viſits, I was very particular in reprefenting their complaints as highly dangerous, and the confequent neceffity for fomebody being appointed to attend them conftantly, in order to adminifter fuch medicines and neceffaries as I ordered; likewife, to fend for me, at leaft, once or twice a day; I, neverthelefs, often had the mortification not to be fent for for two or three days after, and, fometimes, the ftill greater chagrin to find my patient had been entirely neglected, and got beyond the reach of human art to reftore.

This was fo ftrictly the cafe, and attended with fo many diftreffing and fatal confequences, on-board of one fhip in particular, that, for the credit and ſupport of my aſſertions, I ſhall give the circumſtances in detail.

THE Ship I allude to was, at the very point of completing her voyage, caſt away, and unfortunately every ſoul belonging to her periſhed; on which account, it will neither be pleaſant nor proper to diſcloſe names, I ſhall, therefore, only ſay, that, on the arrival of a certain ſhip at Savanna la Marr, I was ſent for to viſit one of her crew, who was ſick.

I found the man in the laſt ſtage of the Yellow Fever, lying in a little, cloſe, and intolerably hot, cabin, between decks. The between-decks, from the ſtern to the main-maſt, which includes the half of the ſpace between decks, was partitioned into ſeveral other little dirty cabins and bed-places, which totally obſtructed the free circulation of air: throughout the other half of the between-decks, alſo in the hold beneath, there was diſtributed a great quantity of filth and rubbiſh, of various kinds, from which there iſſued an intolerable ſtench, ſo that what little air the poor ſick man breathed was ſated with putrid and noxious effluvia.

On enquiring into the cauſe of the ſhip's being in ſuch a foul and lumbered ſtate, between decks, I was informed, that ſhe had been previouſly employed by government, in carrying troops and naval ſtores to one of the Windward-Iſlands; and that they had, ſince then, been ſo hurried and intent on getting down to Savanna la Marr, in due time to load the ſhip, and ſail with the firſt convoy, that time and people could not be ſpared, neither to clean the ſhip nor take down the ſupernumerary cabins and bed-places, that were built for the accommodation of the military paſſengers.

By farther enquiry, I found, that all the crew, conſiſting then of nearly twenty, had been employed in conveying the troops and ſtores on-ſhore; in the performance of which duty, they had been much expoſed to the weather, by night as well as day, and had been guilty of great exceſſes; that they had buried a man of the Yellow Fever before leaving the Windward-Iſlands; and that the man, to whoſe aſſiſtance I was now called, had been taken ſick in the courſe of the ſhip's paſſage to Savanna la Marr.

AFTER giving the neceſſary directions for the management of this ſick man, and ordering him into a more airy ſituation, I waited upon the captain, and repreſented to him, that, from the previous tranſactions of his people to-windward, and the foul ſtate of his ſhip, I was of opinion, that his whole crew would, ſooner or later, be attacked with the Yellow Fever; that the only means by which it could either be prevented or moderated, were to lay the between-decks entirely open, by removing all the ſuperfluous partitions, cabins, and bed-places, ſo as to admit of a free current of air, fore and aft; alſo, to thoroughly clean, fumigate, and lime-whiten, the ſhip, within; and, that the only chance he had of recovering his people, when taken ſick, was inſtantly, to remove them out of the ſhip to a proper houſe on-ſhore, and to provide them in the ſpeedieſt manner the beſt medical aſſiſtance.

THE captain ſeemed alarmed at what I ſaid, and aſſured me that my advice ſhould be ſtrictly followed; but, unfortunately for the crew, his eagerneſs to load the ſhip predominated again very ſoon after I left him.

I was not ſent for regularly, as I deſired, to attend my patient, and he very ſoon died. The ſhip was neglected to be cleared and cleaned, as I directed; and the reſt of the crew, from the captain down to the cabin-boy, were all, in turn, moſt ſeverely attacked by the Yellow Fever.

Even then, no regular mode was adopted, for either his or his people's relief: I was ſent for, to viſit them only once in two or three days, according as the buſineſs of the ſhip permitted, or, as they chanced to be thought of. Some I found lying in the peſtilential air between decks, and others among heaps of rubbiſh and lumber above deck, expoſed to the potent ſun, to rain, and the night-air. They were, alſo, for the moſt part, without any one to attend them, and deſtitute of the common neceſſaries requiſite for their ſupport and reſtoration, and two or three days were often ſuffered to elapſe after I viſited them, before their medicines were ſent for.

At length, a ſecond man dying, and ſeveral of the others appearing likely to follow, the captain yielded to my perſuaſions, and provided a lodging for them on-ſhore; but, they were commonly kept on-board ſo many hours, without any aſſiſtance, after being attacked, and ſo badly attended when on-ſhore, that a third and a fourth man died, and the ſurvivors continued, for a very long time, in a very doubtful ſtate and unfit for duty.

The ſhip's carpenter was one of the ſad victims to negligence, and when he died, in order to ſave time and expence, his corpſe was taken about half a mile from the ſhip, and without the common rites of burial, caſt into the ſea: ſuch a tranſaction, in a civilized and Chriſtian country, and in a place abounding with excellent fiſh, did, as may naturally be imagined, very much diſgrace the captain. I mention this circumſtance meerly to ſhew, that if an hour or two could not be ſpared to perform, in a decent and Chriſtian-like manner, the laſt ſad offices for ſo uſeful and valuable a man as the ſhip's carpenter, what little chance he, or any one elſe on-board, had of being attended with proper care and diligence, through a long and dangerous illneſs.

INFERENCE.

The great number of ſeamen, that the reader will now readily conceive to die, after the manner ſet forth, in this and the preceding ſection, in every iſland, in every port of each iſland, and on-board of almoſt every merchant-ſhip while, in the Weſt-Indies; together with what are impreſſed into the ſhips of war; occaſion the vaſt fleets of merchantmen who annually arrive in, and convey to, the Weſt-Indies, upwards of twenty thouſand ſeamen. to depart, upon an average, with not more than half, or at moſt two-thirds, of the ſeamen that navigated them to the Weſt-Indies.

Some few merchantmen may be conceived to have been firſt manned nearly by apprentices, who are exempt from being impreſſed; others, to have loaded at out-ports, not frequented by ſhips of war, and at too great a diſtance from other ſhipping, for their men to have deſerted, in order to get a great ſum of money for the run-home in other ſhips.

It muſt be acknowledged, that the crews of many ſhips, notwithſtanding the adverſe circumſtances mentioned, continue tolerably healthy; with the far greater number, however, it is commonly otherwiſe, and they will be found returning to Europe with not more than half their original complements of ſeamen; and a few more fortunate may, perhaps, have preſerved two-thirds of their people; but, it is very rare indeed, if a merchant-ſhip perform a voyage to and from the Weſt-Indies, without ſuffering ſome diminution in her crew, either through the Yellow Fever or the vigilance of impreffing officers.

I have dwelt longer on the caufes of the merchant-fhips leaving the Weft-Indies with confiderably lefs men than their original complements confifted of, intentionally to make the matter more clear, and caufe it to be particularly borne in mind, as I fhall have occafion to advert to it hereafter, and in the fequel of my account of the ravages of the Yellow Fever.

SECTION THE THIRD.

Of the production of the Yellow Fever, and confequent lofs of feamen, in the Weft-India merchants' fervice, as ftated in the two preceding fections, the effects of which are not manifeft until they are on their paffage from the Weft-Indies to Europe.

WHEN treating of the nature and caufes of the Yellow Fever, I obferved that, in fome conftitutions, the poifon remained latent, without producing any vifible effects, for many days, and fometimes did not affect feamen until they had got a great way from the Weſt-Indies, and even without the Tropics.

It is my intention, in this place, to ſhew that ſuch is the caſe, and that in conſequence of a vaſt number of ſeamen having been expoſed to, and received the active principle of, the Yellow Fever, in one or other of the ſeveral ways ſet forth in the two preceding ſections, it breaks out among the crews of many Weſt-India and other merchant men, on their homeward paſſages from the Weſt-Indies, and occaſions a farther very conſiderable loſs of ſeamen.

The laſt-mentioned Ship, P-lg--m, having, after the ſale of her ſlaves, at Kingſton, Jamaica, taken up the buſineſs of a Weſt-Indiaman, by going to

Savanna la Marr, and loading with Weſt-Indian produce, ſhe may be conſidered, during that period, as no way differing therefrom, and to have proſecuted her loading, and that part of her voyage, in preciſely the ſame way as Weſt-Indiamen do in general; conſequently, what occurred on board her, and among the ſeamen on her homeward paſſage, may juſtly enough, I preſume, be conſidered as applicable to regular Weſt-Indiamen and their crews, and I ſhall accordingly recite the ſame, in order to prove and elucidate the loſs of ſeamen and other circumſtances before aſſerted.

WHEN our lading was completed, having preſerved only ſeven of our people from being impreſſed and from deſertion, out of thirty-five, which was the number we brought into the Weſt-Indies, the captain engaged ſeven very indifferent ſeamen for fifty guineas each, and one ordinary ſeamen for forty guineas, to work the ſhip home. Theſe eight men were all, as may be well imagined, from the enormous ſums given for their ſervices, in good health, as were, alſo, the older part of the crew, ſo that all hands on-board went to ſea apparently in perfectly good health and ſpirits.

Having met at the general rendezvous and joined the merchantmen from various parts, to the amount of about one hundred and twenty ſail, we, on the 9th day of June, 1796, under the protection of a ſquadron of men of war.

took our departure from the Weſt end of Jamaica.

WHEN we had been about a week at ſea, the Yellow Fever began to affect the crew, particularly thoſe that were engaged by the run, and in about a fortnight, we had eight in a very critical way: this ſickneſs reduced and kept our crew, for ſeveral days, to only ſeven effective men, ſo that the ſhip being very leaky, it was not without great difficulty that ſhe was kept ſufficiently clear of water, to preſerve the cargo from being damaged, and under proper ſail to keep company with the convoy.

OUR people, from the time we left Jamaica, had enjoyed a cool and moderate breeze of wind, with fine clear pleaſant weather; they had alſo been kept very regular and temperate; ſo that there was no apparent nor probable cauſe whatever, for the preſent ſickneſs among them, except their previous expoſure and irregularities on-ſhore, conſequent on their endeavours to avoid being impreſſed, and in getting from other ſhips, at diſtant parts, to engage in the P-lg--m: even the captain and myſelf, who ſince ſailing had been equally regular, as well as better accommodated in ſome reſpects than the people, had an attack of the Yellow Fever, which, like theirs, could not be attributed to any thing but our having been expoſed to the night-air, and inclemencies of the weather, on the ſervice of the ſhip, a little previous to ſailing from Jamaica.

I have often, before, experienced inſtances of the Yellow Fever breaking out among ſlaves, and ſeamen of ſlave-ſhips, ſeveral days after leaving, and after having got a great diſtance from, the Coaſt of Africa, when it could not be in the leaſt accounted for otherwiſe than through infection received on-ſhore anterior to their ſailing. The ſame was, likewiſe, the caſe, among the crews of many of the ſhips compoſing the fleet we accompanied from Jamaica.

THIS very ſurpriſing circumſtance of the Yellow Fever not appearing, nor apparently affecting perſons, for many days, and even months, after expoſure to its cauſes, is noticed, and clearly proved, by Dr. John Hunter, pages 153 and 329 to 335.

OUR ſick at this time, as when the ſhip was loading, were very much diſtreſſed for want of a proper place to repoſe in, the ſhip being ſo fully laden, that there was only a very ſmall ſpace allotted for that purpoſe over the water-caſks between decks, and it was not more than three feet high. To crawl in and out of ſuch a confined ſpot, was not, as will be readily conceived, eaſily done by thoſe that were in health, and was totally out of the power of the ſick: this ſmall ſpace was, moreover, ſo greatly heated by a noxious vapour ariſing from 400 hogſheads of new ſugar that were beneath, and the natural heat of the climate, before we got to the northward of the Tropic of Cancer, that a very ſhort continuance in it occaſioned a difficulty of breathing, and moſt profuſe ſweating, which prevented both ſick and well from occupying it. The vapour or ſteam ariſing from the ſugars ſo diffuſed itſelf throughout the ſhip, and was of ſo penetrating a nature, that it changed the paint-work, in every part and of every colour, black, or, rather, made it look as if it had been ſmeared over with black lead; this happens, more particularly, in damp and rainy weather, and in ſhips, like ours, that were very leaky. Men of medical education will beſt underſtand me when I ſay, that the ſteam from the ſugars made the paint-work look as if the phlogiſton, of former chymiſts, were reſtored to the ſaturnine portion of the paint.

This vapour or ſteam ariſing from new ſugars, when ſuch conſiderable quantities are together on ſhip-board, I have heard ſaid to be productive of the Yellow Fever among ſeamen. The authority was by no means ſufficient to eſtabliſh it as a fact, in my mind, yet, I think, it deſerves particular notice; for, this effluvium is of ſo great annoyance to the ſeamen, both in ſickneſs and health, that, rather than ſubject themſelves to its pernicious influence, within the ſmall ſpace uſually allotted them to ſleep in between-decks, many of them prefer, and, in truth, are ſometimes obliged, to reſt, and take up their conſtant abode, in the open air above deck, expoſed, at ſea as well as in harbour, to the night-air, to dews, to rain, and the ſcorching ſun, which, it is almoſt unneceſſary to remark, cannot prove otherwiſe than injurious to every one, and a frequent cauſe of the Yellow Fever among merchants' ſeamen, when in the Weſt-Indies.

The principal officers of the P-lg--m, as well as myſelf, notwithſtanding our exertions during the ſlaving part of the voyage, and in the loading of the ſhip, the latter of which was an extra piece of ſervice, quite unconnected with our contract for the ſlaving-voyage, as well as a great loſs of time to us, and for all which we received no compenſation, were very little better accommodated, in reſpect to a ſleeping-place, than the ſeamen, which proved very detrimental to our health, and makes the trifling regard paid to the health, comfort, and convenience, of the poor ſeamen the leſs ſurpriſing.

OUR ſick, on account of the confined limits of the place deſigned for their reſt, and the noxious and unbearable heat of it, were obliged, in fact I deſired them as the leaſt evil of the two, to keep night and day upon deck, and to ſcreen themſelves, as well as they could, with their blankets and bedding, from the ſcorching ſun, from rain, and the night-air. The weather, fortunately for them, was in general, for ſome time, very fine and favorable, ſo that, with ſtrict care, they all, except one, recovered, and gave me no farther trouble during the remainder of the voyage.

IN the ſame manner, and from like

causes, did the Yellow Fever, at different periods, affect, to my knowledge, the crews of many of the ships in company. The accommodations of the people for sleeping, whether healthy or sick, were, also, in some instances that I was witness to, no better than ours. And, considering the few hands that the ships in general had to navigate them, it is not to be supposed that a man was allowed, or could, indeed, be spared, to attend them as often as they required. But, what was still more to be lamented, very few indeed of the merchant-ships having surgeons, the sick seamen had in general to struggle through, or die of, their diseases, without medical assistance, or, what was yet worse, to have their complaints aggravated, and perhaps the period of their lives ſhortened, by the taking of improper medicines from the hands of ignorant perſons.

In illuſtration of the laſt circumſtance, I muſt remark, that moſt Weſt-India-men are furniſhed with a medicine-box, out of which the captain or his mate diſpenſe, as they conceive, relief to the ſick when at ſea, and wherever the aſſiſtance of a ſurgeon cannot be obtained. Theſe medicine-boxes are fitted up principally by druggiſts, and ſome few apothecaries, who never experienced, and perhaps even never read a ſingle page of any book on the Yellow Fever, conſequently, the medicines and the directions that are given therewith, muſt be, in general, either of no good effect or productive of evil, which

I know muſt be particularly the caſe, in reſpect to one kind of medicine ſuch boxes always contain, I mean emetics.

Emetics are uſually the firſt things directed, and had recourſe to by the captains and mates of merchantmen, when, at ſuch times as I have mentioned, ſeamen are attacked with the Yellow or Bilious Fever; and I muſt farther remark that ſeamen rarely have any other complaint in the Weſt-Indies.

Now the chief ſymptom and mark of danger, in the Yellow Fever, is an extreme irritability of the ſtomach, which frequently prevents its retaining either food, or drink, or medicine; which is commonly with difficulty allayed, and very often baffles every endeavour, whereby death often ensues. The violent operation of emetics, frequently occasions this very troublesome and fatal sympton, in cases of the Yellow Fever, when it would not otherwise have occurred, and invariably aggravates it when present; therefore, the practice of indiscriminately giving emetics to seamen sick of the Yellow Fever must frequently occasion death, or at best a long and dangerous illness. When, moreover, emetics are not attended with such bad effects, they do not evacuate redundant bile so naturally, pleasantly, nor effectually, as gentle cathartics; on all which accounts, the most judicious of modern practitioners and writers, (see Dr. Hunter's Observations, pages 120, 130, and 315,) proteſt againſt their uſe altogether, in the Yellow Fever.

WHEN the foregoing circumſtances are conſidered, will it be in the leaſt wondered at or otherwiſe than expected that a great number of ſeamen ſhould be taken ſick and die of the Yellow Fever, on their paſſage from the Weſt-Indies. I had, in truth, abundant proof of it, during the whole progreſs of the fleet homewards. In moderate weather, I was ſent for to viſit the ſick on-board other ſhips; and, at times, when a boat could not be ſent for me, merchant-ſhips, having ſick men, were brought within my hearing, for the purpoſe of aſking what ſhould be done for them. The ſtate of health, and number of their crews buried, uſed often to be the firſt queſtions aſked, by captains of merchant-ſhips acquainted with each other, when they got within hail; and many applications were to my knowledge made, by captains of merchantmen, to the commodore of the fleet, for more ſeamen and aſſiſtance, in conſequence of ſickneſs and mortality.

Thus it happens, that very few ſhips, particularly thoſe having runners, perform their paſſages from the Weſt-Indies, without having ſome ſickneſs and looſing a man; others, two or three; and ſome have been known to bury five and even ten; others, again, have had ſuch ſickneſs and mortality, and arrived with their people in ſo deplorable a ſtate, that the officers of health have deemed it neceſſary for them to perform quarantine.

THE ſeamen of the ſhips and fleets that uſually leave the Weſt-Indies in the latter end of July, are always much more ſickly, and commonly a greater number of them die, than in the ſhips and fleets that leave the Weſt-Indies at the time I did, the beginning of the month of June, as before mentioned, which is occaſioned, I conceive, by the ſaid ſeamen committing the irregularities ſpoken of on-ſhore, in the months of June and July, when much rain falls in the Weſt-Indies, which, as was obſerved when treating of the nature and cauſes of the Yellow Fever, gives additional power and virulence to the effluvia that occaſion it.

I have heard the ſickneſs and mortality among the ſeamen of the ſhips and fleets that ſail laſt in the ſeaſon, from Jamaica, ſpoken of as very great and ſhocking indeed, and to ſatisfy the reader, in ſome degree, of the truth thereof, I ſhall beg his attention to the following lamentable facts, which were lately related to me by an officer in the Weſt-India trade who witneſſed them.

THE Ship D-ke of Cl-r--ce, of L-nd-n, Captain C-b-ld, ſailed from Jamaica, on the 25th of July, 1794, in company with a large fleet of merchantmen; her crew conſiſted of eighteen people, and they were all apparently in perfect health: on the 30th of the ſame month ſeven of them were taken ſick of the Yellow Fever, and the next day, dreadful and aſtoniſhing to relate, they all died. About the ſame time, the Ship C-rl--le, of L-nd-n, Captain B-yd-n, loſt nine of her crew by the Yellow Fever within three days; and many of the other ſhips compoſing the fleet loſt one, two, three, and even four, of their people in the ſame manner.

In ſhort, the ſickneſs I have repreſented, and endeavoured to account for, is ſo common, well known, and much expected, that it is now thought requiſite, and become regular, for the captains of Weſt-Indiamen, particularly thoſe from Jamaica, on their arrival home, to report to proper health-officers, appointed for that purpoſe, the ſtate of the health of their crews, that, in caſe of ſickneſs, the neceſſary ſteps may be taken to prevent the propagation of the Yellow Fever on-ſhore.

SEAMEN's exacting and captains' promiſing ſuch great ſums of money, as I have mentioned, for the bare taſk of working a ſhip from the Weſt-Indies to Europe, occaſions a deal of litigation between the commanders of Weſt-India merchantmen and ſeamen, on their arrival home, and tends to create and maintain a ſpirit of animoſity which is, I am afraid, very unfavorable to the ſeamen's obtaining ſuch indulgencies when ſick as they require, and which their captains would otherwiſe, perhaps, be inclined to grant them: I have, in truth, obſerved too much of it, towards thoſe ſeamen I have had the care of, and ſhall juſt recite one inſtance to that effect. A ſhip of the fleet I came laſt from Jamaica with, in the early part of the paſſage, loſt one of her men, a runner, at fifty guineas, by the Yellow Fever; ſoon after committing the body to the deep, the captain of the ſaid ſhip got cloſe to another, commanded by an acquaintance, who aſked him what news, and how all fared on-board? when, inſtead of expreſſing a concern for the loſs of a valuable man to his ſhip and country, he inſtantly replied, in an ironical and joyful tone, that he had juſt thrown fifty guineas overboard; and concluded his explanation, by expreſſing a concern at not being likely to get rid of any more of the impoſing raſcals in the ſame way.

SECTION THE FOURTH.

Of the loſs and ſufferings of ſeamen, in the Weſt-India merchants' ſervice, through the want of proper medical and ſurgical aſſiſtance, when they are affected with the venereal diſeaſe and have received accidents.

MANY ſeamen are neceſſitated, through the want of money to pay a ſurgeon, and to ſupport themſelves on-ſhore until they are cured of the venereal diſeaſe, to go to ſea, in merchant-men, from both the Weſt-Indies and Europe, when affected with the venereal diſeaſe, particularly, of that ſtage of it called a clap; and others departing ſoon after connexion with infected women, have venereal complaints break out upon them after they get to ſea.

From theſe circumſtances, many ſeamen are induced to enter on-board African ſlave-ſhips, who, but for the benefit of the ſurgeon's aſſiſiſtance, would not even think of encountering with the more than common hardſhips and perils attendant on a ſlaving voyage.

Most Weſt Indiamen, as I before obſerved, are provided with medicine-boxes, fitted up principally by druggiſts, who have not had a medical education, and they uſually contain an ample ſtock of medicines for the cure of the venereal diſeaſe, which are compofed chiefly of mercury, and that fometimes in too active forms and dofes, and which the captain or his mate ignorantly difpenfe among fuch feamen as are found to be in need, when at fea: feamen themfelves, alfo, take medicines of the like nature, and for the fame purpofes, privately to fea with them, from quacks, and other pretenders to cure the venereal difeafe.

I have often been fent for on-board merchantmen, to vifit feamen affected with this difeafe, and have, confequently, had opportunities of examining feveral of their medicine-boxes, and the medicines otherwife fupplied to feamen; whence I know, and conceive myfelf authorized to affert, that the medicines, and directions that are given therewith, are, oftentimes, improper, and, in ſome ſtages of the venereal diſeaſe, highly dangerous; conſequently, that the ſeamen ſo affected, muſt ſuffer greatly in their conſtitutions, either through having no aſſiſtance at all, or that which muſt frequently prove ineffectual or dangerous.

This will appear particularly clear and forcible to medical readers, who know the uncontroulable and deſtructive nature of that diſeaſe, and the almoſt ungovernable and pernicious effects of mercury, in ſome conſtitutions, even when beſt accommodated and under the management of the moſt ſkilful: what, then, but the very worſt effects, is to be looked for, when they influence perſons like ſeamen, expoſed to all vicissitudes of weather and climate, and when, as I have shewn, they either have none, or only the most ignorant of the venereal disease and of its remedies, to direct for them.

On my last passage from the West-Indies, I was sent for from merchant-men, even at sea, to visit seamen affected with this disease. The situation and sufferings of one poor fellow were such as I cannot reflect upon without pain: I found him lying on the upper deck, greatly emaciated and worn out, through discharge and pain, from a large ulcer and two buboes.

Here was a case very flagrantly maltreated, and now requiring the most skilful management. He had taken, by his account, a deal of medicine, from the captain and mate, now, moſt evidently, to no good purpoſe. Unfortunately, the weather became ſo unfavorable, that I could not viſit him a ſecond time; and as to the event of his diſorder, I never could learn: moſt likely, however, by committing himſelf again into the hands of his former phyſicians, the captain and mate, or, through not having any aſſiſtance at all, for a conſiderable time after I ſaw him, and till the ſhip arrived in England, either death or irreparable injury to his conſtitution muſt have been the conſequence.

ALMOST all Weſt-Indiamen, but particularly the larger, carry a number of guns and ſmall arms in war time, to defend themſelves from the enemy;

among accidents, therefore, may, properly enough, be included all ſuch wounds and hurts as ſeamen are liable to receive in the defence of their ſhips, as well as what happen to them from burns, ſcalds, falls into their ſhip's hold and from aloft, alſo, in the loading and unloading of their ſhips, and ſuſpenſion of life from falling into the water; to all which, ſo great a body of ſeamen as I am treating of muſt, in a very conſiderable degree, be ſubjected; and which, for want of proper medical and ſurgical aſſiſtance, muſt often end either in the loſs of life, incurable lameneſs, or degeneracy into bad ulcers, which render them, for a great length of time, unſerviceable to their ſhips, and often, in the end, occaſion the neceſſity of amputation.

MANY inſtances of the kind have come to my knowledge, four of which I ſhall particularize, and they, the more unfortunately, happened to be fine ſeamen in the meridian of life.

FIRST.—On my paſſage from Africa to the Weſt-Indies, in the Sl--p Sw-ft, before-mentioned, we fell in company with a merchant-ſhip bound home from the South-Sea whale-fiſhery, having been abſent thirteen months: early in the voyage, one of her crew, by accident, diſlocated his ſhoulder, and, by the time I ſaw him, the ſeveral parts compoſing that articulation had conformed ſo much to the change, that his arm could not be replaced, whereby he was diſabled from ſerving his country during the reſt of his life.

SECOND. — Captain W-ll--ms, of the Ship H-rm-t, of Br-ſt l, on a paſſage to the Weſt-Indies, in 1794, having occaſion to ſcale his guns, a ſeaman very imprudently placed himſelf before one of them, directly after being fired off, in order to recharge it, and probably without previouſly ſponging the gun out, he put therein a full charge of powder, which he drove home, with one end of the rammer placed againſt his breaſt; when done, before he could either withdraw the rammer or get from the front of the gun, the powder caught fire, through ſome ſparks that were left within the breech of the gun, by the former cartridge, and, in an inſtant of time, he was driven from the gun into atoms, and nothing of him could be diſcovered afterwards but a very ſmall piece of his apparel. Had this unfortunate man placed himſelf, as he ought, by the ſide of the gun to ram home the charge, one or both of his arms would have been blown off or ſhattered to pieces, in which caſe, there being no ſurgeon at hand to ſtop a bleeding artery, to ſeparate mangled parts, or to amputate if neceſſary, he muſt inevitably have died, or remained a ſhocking ſpectacle until the ſhip arrived in the Weſt-Indies.

I have known three ſeamen looſe their arms, and one his leg, on-board armed merchantmen, when only firing ſalutes. How lamentable muſt be the conſequence of an armed merchantman, not having a ſurgeon on-board, fighting a long and deſperate battle!

THIRD.—William Saunders, as fine a North-country ſeaman as ever I beheld, and in the very prime of life, preſented himſelf at the London-Hoſpital for relief, in February, 1797. Coming home from Jamaica, late in the year 1796, on-board the Ship Alb--n, of N-wc---le, Captain H-nn-ck, one of his legs was broken by a puncheon of rum, which was ſtowed above deck, breaking looſe and rolling againſt him, during a hard gale of wind; and, for want of ſurgical aſſiſtance, his leg was united in a moſt frightful and diſtorted manner: the callous, or medium of union, for want, alſo, of proper treatment, was ſo ſuperabundant as to form a large tumor at the fore and lateral parts of his leg, which diſplaced all the moving powers of the limb from their proper ſpheres of action, whereby the man loſt the uſe of his leg entirely, and was rendered unſerviceable to his country, as a ſeaman, for life.

THIS man informed me, that moſt of his ſhip-mates ran away on the ſhip's arrival at Port-Morant, Jamaica, where ſhe was loaded; that her crew were four leſs in number on her homeward than on her outward paſſage; that he was often obliged, as were alſo the ſeamen belonging to other ſhips in company, to be away two days and nights at a time, in open boats, fetching fugars; that there was a very great mortality among the feamen belonging to the fhips that loaded in company with his: in fome, he faid, three and four, in others five and fix, died of the Yellow Fever; and, that his berth between decks, was too confined and hot to be flept in during the firft part of the fhip's paffage home, there being only juft room left to fqueeze in, above fome cafks of rum, as may be judged from my preceding account of rum being ftowed above deck.

FOURTH.—William Johnfon, a black native of America, coming from Jamaica to England, in June, 1796, on-board the Ship Br-ckw--d, of L-nd-n, Captain F-g-y, received a hurt on one of his legs, which, for want of proper ſurgical aſſiſtance, ſoon became ſo bad as to prevent his doing any duty during a great part of the ſhip's paſſage home, and occaſioned a very extenſive caries, or rottenneſs of the bone, on account of which he was admitted into the London-Hoſpital, and at length obliged to undergo amputation of the leg.

By this man's account, afterwards, he received no ſmart-money, from the merchants and owners of the ſhip, on account of looſing a leg in their ſervice; nor even payment of the ſum for which he was engaged to work during the ſhip's run-home; and was told, when he made application for his run-money, that, inftead of receiving any thing, he ought to pay for the provifions he ate while incapable of doing his duty.

THE number of merchantmen, of every defcription, I have treated of, as going to and from the Weft-Indies, and not having furgeons on-board, I fhall next endeavour to fhew to be very great.

SECTION THE FIFTH.

Circumſtances that may be adduced by others, as tending to leſſen and ameliorate the before-ſaid loſs and ſufferings of ſeamen in the Weſt-India merchants' ſervice; but which are not of ſuch extenſive benefit as is imagined.

THE number of Britiſh merchantmen that go annually, from different parts, and for different purpoſes, to the Weſt-Indies, I have ſaid to be about a thouſand ſail, and that they employ upwards of twenty thouſand ſeamen: three-fourths of this number of ſhipping

I have, alſo, ſaid to be compoſed of Weſt-Indiamen, or ſugar-ſhips; and, that among the other fourth, are, ſome from Newfoundland and North-America: now, I will be bold to ſay, that not more than one in an hundred of thoſe different ſhips carry a ſurgeon, and ſuch as do, it is chiefly for the benefit of paſſengers. The African ſlave-ſhips, do all of them carry a ſurgeon at firſt ſailing from England; but, it is greatly to be lamented, that, nearly half of them die, before thoſe ſhips reach the Weſt-Indies; and there again ſome die; and others, through advantageous opportunities of ſettling, diſguſt, or ill treatment, leave their ſhips in the Weſt-Indies: ſo that, as I have not included in my account any loſs or ſufferings among ſeamen in African ſlave-ſhips, of which, alas, there is but too much, before their arrival in the Weſt-Indies, they will then be found but little better provided with ſurgeons than any of the other deſcription of veſſels: thus, about nine-tenths of the whole number of ſhipping will be found, within the period of their voyages to and from the Weſt-Indies, without ſurgeons, and the vaſt body of ſeamen they employ, however grievouſly and extenſively afflicted, when at ſea, without the poſſibility of obtaining any medical or ſurgical help.

SUCH being the deplorable ſituation of Weſt-India merchants' ſeamen, in general, with reſpect to medical and ſurgical aſſiſtance, when traverſing the ſeas, and while, as I have ſhewn, they are liable to much ſickneſs and various miſhaps, I ſhall next ſtate how it fares with them, in thoſe reſpects, while in the Weſt-Indies, where, as I have repreſented, they are ſubject to ſtill more ailment, and where there is a much greater number liable to be affected by ſickneſs, and, conſequently, requiring aſſiſtance.

It is uſual for the regular Weſt-Indiamen to pay a ſurgeon ſo much money, the ſum, I believe, is ten pounds, each voyage, to attend their ſeamen and find them medicines, while in the Weſt-Indies. Great and many are the inconveniences and evils attending this practice! The Yellow Fever, as I before observed, is almost the only complaint that affects seamen in the West-Indies; and such is its insidious and malignant nature, that unless the physician is called early, attends most assiduously, and manages very skilfully, little will his visits avail. The West-India physicians and surgeons regard the business of attending ships in such, manner, in the light in which medical men in this country consider attendance on poor-houses, as very inferior practice and but little worth their notice; they will not, therefore, nor can indeed at all times, seasons, and distances, go on-board ships so speedily, regularly, and often, as required.

On the part of the ſhip it, likewiſe, often happens, either through hurry of buſineſs, not conceiving a man to be really ſick, not having a boat and hands on-board, through diſtance, or unfavorableneſs of weather, that the ſurgeon is not, nor can be, ſent for, before the ſick are in the greateſt danger, and even paſt recovery: from the ſame circumſtances, it is too often the caſe too, that, for want of having medicines ſpeedily and regularly, and of ſomebody to ſee them faithfully adminiſtered, thoſe whoſe complaints, at firſt, were but trifling, do alſo ſlip off the ſtage of life.

Sick ſeamen are ſometimes removed out of their ſhips to the ſhore, for the ſake of better attendance and accommodation; but it is, in general, done at very late and improper periods; they are alſo, commonly, on ſuch occaſions, put under the care of negro-women, who have neither authority nor power to make them take their medicines regularly, nor to reſtrain them from drinking, and other abuſes of themſelves, when they are a little recovered; and the payment of ſuch perſons as undertake the care of ſick ſeamen is, likewiſe, precarious and trifling; on which accounts, the ſeamen are ſeldom much, if at all, better off than when ſick on ſhip-board.

Of the loſs and ſufferings of ſeamen, through ſuch neglect, and want of proper attendance, accommodation, and medical aſſiſtance, I have before treated very fully, and even exhibited proofs, as the reader will see, pages 60 to 70: very little enquiry will, I am certain, farther prove that many seamen die, of the Yellow Fever, through the like means and neglect, on-board of such West-Indiamen as do constantly, when in the West-Indies, pay and employ a surgeon.

The venereal disease and accidents are seldom or never, I believe, included in the surgeon's contract, but to be paid for separately, by the respective persons who may happen to be so afflicted: the captains of merchantmen, on account of the uncertainty of seamen's continuance with them in the West-Indies, very often will not advance, nor be answerable for the payment of, what may be required on ſuch occaſions; through which, and the conſequent neglect, ſlight complaints often become great and ſerious, and the ſeamen again ſuffer very materially.

As to the medicine-boxes, taken to ſea in merchantmen, according to their preſent plan, and the uſe made of them, as I have repreſented, pages 87 to 90, and 97 to 102, they muſt be conſidered rather of evil than benefit to the ſeamen.

The few ſurgeons that remain in the African ſlave-ſhips, but a little while after their arrival in the Weſt-Indies; the ſtill fewer that are to be found in any of the other deſcription of veſſels; the employment of ſurgeons; and the ſending of ſick ſeamen on-ſhore, in the Weſt-Indies, in the way here treated of; are the only circumſtances, within my knowledge and recollection, at preſent exiſting, that can be by others adduced or ſuppoſed, in the ſmalleſt degree, either to leſſen or ameliorate the loſs and ſufferings I have repreſented to happen among ſeamen in the Weſt-India merchants' ſervice: the inconſiderableneſs of their effect, the reader muſt now, I am ſure, with me, deplore.

THE THIRD PART.

CAUSES OF THE LOSS OF SEAMEN ON-BOARD SHIPS OF WAR ON THE WEST-INDIA STATION.

THE loſs of ſeamen is here again occaſioned by the Yellow Fever, in conſequence of impreſſing ſeamen on-ſhore, and out of merchantmen, in the Weſt-Indies; through, alſo, improper medical treatment of the Fever; and through the want of a ſufficient quantity of the Peruvian Bark.

SECTION THE FIRST.

Of the production of the Yellow Fever, and consequent loss of seamen, on-board ships of war on the West-India station, through impressing seamen on-shore, and out of merchantmen.

I Have, page 71, particularly noticed the merchantmen leaving the West-Indies with not more, upon an average, than half, or at most two-thirds, of the seamen that navigated them thereto; the deficiency I stated to be occasioned by death, through the Yellow Fever, and their being impressed into the ships of war: it is here neceſſary, to ſhew, farther, that ſuch only are the ſources of the deficiency.

THE ſame vigilance is practiſed by the men of war in impreſſing Britiſh ſeamen out of American merchantmen, and thoſe of other nations at peace with us, on their arrival in, and departure from, any of our Weſt-India iſlands, as is exerciſed among our own merchantmen; ſo that, whatever lure may be thrown out, or encouragement given, for ſeamen to leave our ſhips in the Weſt-Indies, and enter into thoſe of other nations, they have very little chance of getting clear away, at leaſt, not in any conſiderable number; and thoſe that do are, I conceive, nearly if not quite equalled, in number, by the Britiſh and American ſeamen that the ſhips of war impreſs out of American and other merchantmen, on their arrival in the Weſt-Indies.

FARTHER, as to any employment that our ſeamen can get in the Weſt-Indies, otherwiſe than in the Britiſh merchantmen, it is ſo very inconſiderable as hardly to deſerve notice. The navigation from iſland to iſland, and from port to port of the ſame iſland, of droghers, as they are called, or ſuch veſſels as properly belong to the Weſt-Indies, is done almoſt entirely by mulattoes and blacks. But very few privateers are equipped in the Weſt-Indies, and they, alſo, bear a great many mulattoes and blacks, and the ſeamen that are beſides employed therein, muſt, at the end of their reſpečtive cruizes, either return into ſome one or other of the Britiſh merchantmen or become impreſſed.

THUS, it comes out, that ſuch ſeamen as do not die on-ſhore, nor on-board the merchantmen, after the manner deſcribed, and who go to form the other part of the deficiency in their crews, at their departure from the Weſt-Indies, do all, ſooner or later, become impreſſed into the ſhips of war.

SOME of them, as I before obſerved, are caught immediately on their arrival in the Weſt-Indies, and, conſequently, before being at all expoſed on-ſhore, whereby they eſcape the Yellow Fever; and, through the clean, regular, and temperate, conduct, they are obliged to adhere to on-board ſhips of war, if they are not ſent on either the impreſs, or other duty on-ſhore, their health continues, for the moſt part, uninterrupted, during the whole of their ſtay in the Weſt-Indies.

Others, through the extreme vigilance of the impreſſing-gangs, are from time to time taken, either on-ſhore or out of the merchantmen, after having been, for ſome time, at hide and ſeek, and abuſing their conſtitutions, on-ſhore: the people ſo taken, together with thoſe that are employed in impreſſing them who, when on ſuch ſervice, are often, through neceſſity, expoſed to the night-air, to dews, to rain, and the burning ſun, and who are, alſo, diſpoſed to drunkenneſs, are many of them, within a few days afterwards, attacked with the Yellow Fever; and ſo, as the impreſſing duty goes on, there is an almoſt conſtant ſucceſſion of ſickneſs kept up, on-board ſome of our ſhips of war.

Thus, impreſſing ſeamen on-ſhore, and out of merchantmen, in the Weſt-Indies. becomes the chief cauſe of the introduction of the Yellow Fever into ſhips of war on the Weſt-India ſtation, and occaſions ſuch a loſs of ſeamen, that, notwithſtanding the vaſt number that are annually impreſſed, many of the ſhips of war, as well as merchantmen, will be found to leave the Weſt-Indies, at the end of their reſpective ſtations, with not more, and ſome having even far leſs, men than they brought therein: it ſometimes happens even in ſhips of war that have not lent any aid to others, nor been in any engagement, nor in any hazardous enterprize, whereby a number of men could have been ſwept away.

But it is more particularly the caſe on-board ſuch ſhips of war as have occaſional drafts of men made from them into other ſhips, or to man prizes, and, in conſequence, are obliged to have recourſe to impreſſing to keep up their complements: alſo, on-board ſuch ſhips as are taken from the enemy, and put into commiſſion in the Weſt Indies, and, of courſe, muſt be manned, nearly if not entirely, by impreſſing.

I ſaw ſome woeful examples of theſe practices, during the American war, among the French prizes, taken in the Weſt-Indies, by Lord Rodney, in the month of April, 1782. I was appointed to ſerve as a ſurgeon's mate, on-board one of them, the Le Caton, of 64 guns, ſoon after they were brought into Port-Royal, Jamaica, which ſhip was manned as I have deſcribed, that is, ſufficiently for being brought into port and navigated home, by ſmall drafts of chiefly newly-impreſſed men, from other ſhips concer ed in her capture, and by now and then impreſſing a few on-ſhore, and out of the merchantmen. A very few days after my going on-board, the Yellow Fever broke out among the crew, and even affected the officers; and during the three months that we ſtaid at Port Royal, it raged with violence equal to a plague. The reſt of the prizes, being manned in the ſame manner, were all equally ſickly, and dreadful indeed was the mortality in all.

THE introduction of the Yellow Fever into ſhips of war on the Weſt-India ſtation, in the manner here ſet forth, is, alſo, noticed by Dr. John Hunter; ſee his Obſervations, page 108.

SECTION THE SECOND.

Of the loſs of ſeamen on-board ſhips of war on the Weſt-India ſtation, through improper medical treatment of the Yellow Fever.

MY experience and practice of late days have proved to me, that the ſick of the Yellow Fever, on-board ſhips of war on the Weſt-India ſtation, at leaſt, in ſome of the ſhips that I ſerved in, ſuffered very materially from improper medical treatment.

UNDER the idea that redundant bile was the primary cauſe of the Yellow

Fever, and of its moſt diſtreſſing and frequently fatal ſymptom, an extreme irritability of the ſtomach which prevents its retaining either food or medicine, it was the practice of many naval ſurgeons, in the days I ſerved in the Royal Navy, to adminiſter very powerful antimonial emetics, and even to repeat them again and again, if the ſtomach continued to eject bile or remained unſettled.

I have often, in conſequence of ſuch treatment, ſeen ſeamen ſick of the Yellow Fever, kept for hours, in the ſhip's head, under the violent operation of emetics, and not unfrequently, at the ſame time, expoſed to either the midday ſun or the chilling and noxious evening air, whereby they have been greatly weakened and their complaints confiderably aggravated; and which now clearly accounts to me for the very violent fpafms of the ftomach, inceffant ficknefs, and exceffive bilious vomitings, with which many of them were afterwards affected, that were always with extreme difficulty allayed, and that fometimes baffled every endeavour.

This rude treatment, together with waiting for a complete intermiffion of the Fever, as was, alfo, the practice, at that time, occafioned a neglect, and too often an utter impracticabilty, of adminiftering the Peruvian Bark, on the early and liberal exhibition of which the recovery of perfons affected by the Yellow Fever, chiefly depends.

It really concerns me when I reflect on the many feamen, within my knowledge, whofe lives might probably have been preferved, by firft a cathartic or two, to caufe the redundant bile to flow gently, and with as little agitation as poffible, through its natural channel downwards, and, at the fame time, relieve the veffels of the abdominal vifcera from morbid fullnefs; by, alfo, a moderate ufe of opium, to appeafe mental inquietude and the particular irritability of the ftomach; and, next, by an early, affiduous, and free, ufe of the Peruvian Bark, to give the whole fyftem ftrength to overcome the effects of the univerfally irritating miafmata, alfo, to impart tone to the veffels of the abdominal vifcera, and enable them to contract againft any farther preternatural flow of fluids into them, and thereby permanently obviate undue ſecretion of bile.

THE bad effects of emetics, and great efficacy of the Peruvian Bark, in the Yellow Fever, are, likewiſe, aſſerted and maintained by Dr. John Hunter: ſee his Obſervations, pages 88, 120, 130, and 315.

SECTION THE THIRD.

Of the loſs of ſeamen, in ſhips of war on the Weſt-India ſtation, through the want of a ſufficient quantity of the Peruvian Bark, for the relief of the ſick of the Yellow Fever.

AT the period of time mentioned in the laſt ſection, ſuch naval ſurgeons on the Weſt-India ſtation, of whom there no doubt were many, who from education and experience, were well aware of the danger of the former, and the benefit of the latter, mode of treating the Yellow Fever, had it not in their power to relieve the ſick in a manner equal to their ſkill and wiſhes: their allowance from government to ſupply medicines was not ſufficient for them to provide a proper quantity of that invaluable medicine, the Peruvian Bark, for ordinary and moderate degrees of prevalence of the Yellow Fever, much leſs, may it be ſuppoſed, when that diſeaſe raged for a continuance, through the greater part of a ſhip's company and a large fleet, as I have known it to do, and often does, from other cauſes beſides thoſe it has been my object more particularly to point out.

The uſual price of a pound of Bark, in the Weſt-Indies, uſed to be, in thoſe times, about twenty ſhillings ſterling; and when it was ſcarce, or much ſickneſs prevailed, I have known it as high as two guineas per pound; ſo that, it often happened, the more occaſion the ſurgeons of ſhips of war had for the Peruvian Bark, the leſs they were enabled to obtain a ſufficient quantity of it to relieve the ſick: thus, ſurgeons who were very well ſkilled in the treatment of the Yellow Fever, from not having the means of relief within their reach, had the mortification and diſcredit of looſing many of their patients, as well as thoſe that were inexperienced; the effects of which cauſes, among the ſeamen of ſo great a fleet as is commonly ſtationed in the Weſt-Indies, during war, when the vaſt prevalence of the Yellow Fever is conſidered, muſt, I am confident, have been very conſiderable indeed.

THE vaſt dearneſs of Peruvian Bark in the Weſt-Indies, alſo, the very extenſive demand for it on-board ſhips of war on the Weſt-India ſtation, and the inadequateneſs of the ſurgeon's allowance, from goverment, to the ſupply of a ſufficient quantity for the relief of the ſick of the Yellow Fever, which I have repreſented, are, alſo, noticed by Dr. John Hunter: ſee his Obſervations, page 110.

FROM all enquiries which I was enabled to make, when laſt in the Weſt-Indies, I found, that the Yellow Fever was ſtill treated, by ſome naval ſurgeons, after the improper manner I have ſet forth; that a liberal uſe of the Peruvian Bark was by many others deemed abſolutely requiſite to the recovery of ſeamen ſick of the Yellow Fever; and that there then exiſted the ſame want and nearly the ſame dearneſs of that medicine; conſequently, the ſame loſs of ſeamen happens now through ſuch cauſes, as when I ſerved in the Royal Navy.

THE FOURTH PART.

OF THE BEFORE-SAID LOSS OF SEAMEN HAPPENING, BOTH IN SHIPS OF WAR AND MERCHANTMEN, CHIEFLY DURING WAR. — OF THE AGGREGATE OF THE LOSS BEING, AS SAID, FIVE THOUSAND ANNUALLY; AND, THE MEANS BY WHICH IT MAY BE MORE CERTAINLY AND SATISFACTORILY ASCERTAINED.

WHEN we are at peace with other nations, ſeamen are very plentiful in the Weſt-Indies; conſequently, there is no ſuch extraordinary ſums of money, as I have reprefented, either afked for or given to them, for working merchantmen home; there is then, alfo, but few fhips of war in the Weft-Indies, and they have little or no occafion to imprefs feamen from the merchantmen: the feamen, therefore, in both fhips of war and merchantmen, not having either the pecuniary inducement to defert, nor a prefs-gang to fly from, do more commonly content themfelves on-board their refpective fhips, and conform to a more regular and fober performance of their duties; under which favorable circumftances, agreeably to the principles laid down when treating of the nature and caufes of the Yellow Fever, and barring the boating and watering duties, alfo, their intemperances when on-fhore for their own recreation or otherwiſe, and their want of a proper ſleeping-place in the merchant-ſervice, they do, in general, enjoy as good health in the Weſt-Indies as in any other part of the world.

When the reader reflects on the vaſt number of ſeamen that the merchantmen annually convey to the Weſt-Indies, which I have ſaid to be upwards of twenty thouſand; and, on the circumſtance of both ſhips of war and merchantmen, but more particularly the latter, leaving the Weſt-Indies with conſiderably leſs men than their original complements; when, likewiſe, he adverts to the mortality on-board the merchantmen, on their homeward paſſages; he muſt be very clearly and forcibly ſtruck with the greatneſs of the loſs of ſeamen, by the Yellow Fever, through the ſeveral means I have repreſented; and will, I dare ſay, be inclined to credit my opinion and eſtimate of its not being leſs than five thouſand annually.

Fully impreſſed, as I am, with the boldneſs, the importance, and the truth, of what I have committed to paper, I cannot otherwiſe than feel myſelf concerned at not being able to aſcertain the preciſe extent of the loſs of ſeamen, through the ſeveral means I have repreſented, and at not having more pointed proof of its being deſerving the attention of the moſt illuſtrious, right honourable, and reſpectable, perſonages to whom I have preſumed to addreſs myſelf; but, that it really is ſo, and little, if any, ſhort of what I have computed it, I am firm in my opinion and confident of, and I feel no ſmall ſatisfaction in being able to ſhew the means by which the ſaid loſs and ſufferings of ſeamen, in both ſhips of war and merchantmen, may be more clearly and ſatisfactorily aſcertained.

THE deſertion of ſeamen from one merchantman to another, in order to obtain large ſums of money for the run-home from the Weſt-Indies; their leaving their ſhips, and going on-ſhore, to avoid being impreſſed; their expoſure to the cauſes of the Yellow Fever in the boating duty; their diſorderly conduct when, on thoſe ſeveral occaſions, they are on-ſhore; the badneſs of their accommodations both in health and ſickneſs; their want of proper medical aſſiſtance and attendance; the numbers buried on-ſhore, and from the merchantmen, while in the Weſt-Indies, as well as on their paſſages to Europe; together with the numbers impreſſed into the ſhips of war; may be all thoroughly known from the commanders of Weſt-Indiamen, and by inſpecting their muſter-rolls; alſo, by referring to the parochial books in the Weſt-Indies, which could be eaſily done through the medium of the different cuſtom-houſes here and in the Weſt-Indies.

THE books of ſhips of war on the Weſt-India ſtation will ſhew that a great many ſeamen annually deſert, and that, moſt probably, as I have ſaid, for the purpoſes of obtaining large ſums of money for the run-home in merchantmen; alſo, that a vaſt number are yearly impreſſed on-ſhore and out of merchantmen; likewiſe, what have died within a few days after being ſo impreſſed, which will afford a preſumptive proof of ſuch deaths having been occaſioned by previous expoſure to the cauſes of the Yellow Fever; and, that, notwithſtanding ſuch continual recruit from the merchantmen, the deaths, from cauſes unconnected with the misfortunes of war, are ſo numerous, as to cauſe many of them to leave the Weſt-Indies with not more, and even leſs, men than their original complements.

The evidence and opinions of ſome

able and intelligent naval ſurgeons, who have ſerved on the Weſt-India ſtation, would, I dare ſay, be found to correſpond with what I have ſaid, on the introduction of the Yellow Fever on board ſhips of war, through the impreſs ſervice; alſo, on their different modes of treating that diſeaſe; and, on the great efficacy of the Peruvian Bark, as well as their inability to furniſh a ſufficient quantity of that medicine for the relief of the ſick of the Yellow Fever.

SHOULD the naval ſurgeons, however, not think proper to make ſuch confeſſion, or differ from me in their opinion, what is ſtated, in thoſe reſpects, by Dr. John Hunter, in the ſeveral pages of his treatiſe "On the Diſeaſe of the Army, in Jamaica," which I have already referred the reader to, will ſurely have ſuperior weight, and be a ſufficient teſt and authority for the truth of what I have aſſerted, as well as ſome excuſe for my preſuming to comment on the medical practice of naval ſurgeons and the medical appointments of ſo great a navy.

THE loſs of ſeamen, and the irreparable injury which the conſtitutions of many of them ſuffer, in the Weſt-India merchants' ſervice, through the want of medical aſſiſtance, when they are affected with the venereal diſeaſe and have received accidents, do not, nor can in their nature, ſtrike the public mind ſo often, ſo clearly, or ſo forcibly, as the loſs, and their ſufferings, through the Yellow Fever; but, an examination of the different Weſt-India merchantmen's muſter-rolls; alſo, an enquiry into, and a regiſter kept of, all the ſeamen received into the ſeveral hoſpitals of the three kingdoms, on ſuch accounts, for only one year, would, I am certain, prove them to be deſerving the moſt ſerious attention.

RETROSPECT.

HERE let me intreat the reader to reflect on the many centuries that England has been preserved from the fury of mighty and implacable foes, through the skill and bravery of her seamen; and how singularly they have added to her security and glory of late: the retrospect will surely excite, in the breast of every Englishman, the most grateful sentiments, and incline him to compassion and benevolence towards a class of people so highly deserving and necessary to our existence as a nation:

ſuch impreſſions never ought to be, nor ever will, I truſt, become effaced; but will, I hope, incline the whole of my readers, moſt joyfully with me, in the next place, to the ſerious conſideration of the means which I ſhall propoſe, to obviate the vaſt loſs and ameliorate the ſufferings, which I have repreſented to happen among ſeamen in the Weſt-India merchants' ſervice, and on board ſhips of war on the Weſt-India ſtation.

THE FIFTH PART.

MEANS OF PREVENTING AND AMELIORATING THE BEFORE-SAID LOSS AND SUFFERINGS OF SEAMEN IN THE WEST-INDIA MERCHANTS' SERVICE.

THE reader will, I dare ſay, anticipate me in the means I have to propoſe, for the accompliſhment of the above moſt deſirable purpoſes, namely, regulating their wages and preventing them from deſertion; aboliſhing the impreſs ſervice in the Weſt-Indies, or elſe, preventing ſeamen from leaving their ſhips, and going on-ſhore, in the Weſt-Indies, to avoid being impreſſed: keeping them as much as can be on-board their ſhips, and when they muſt of neceſſity go on-ſhore, on their ſhip's duty or otherwiſe, ſheltering them, as much as practicable, from the night-air and inclemencies of the weather; alſo, allowing them a proper place to ſleep in on-board; and providing them, in the ſpeedieſt manner, the beſt medical and ſurgical aſſiſtance, as well as requiſite attendance, when they are ſick and have received accidents.

SECTION THE FIRST.

Of regulating merchants' ſeamen's wages, and preventing them from deſertion, in order to their preſervation from the Yellow Fever.

THE proper ſtandards for regulating the wages of ſeamen in the merchants' ſervice are, I conceive, their different degrees of uſefulneſs in their profeſſion; alſo, what the times may require for the equipment of them for ſea, and the maintenance of their families; and, laſtly, the nature, as well as peril, of the ſervices they are, at different times, and in different places, required to perform.

In war time, they have the additional and perilous taſk of defending their ſhips from the enemy, and run the riſk of being, thereby, killed, wounded, or maimed for life; alſo, of being taken priſoner, and experiencing the inſults, the barbarities, and the plundering habits, of conquering enemies; the loſs of time, the loſs of health, and the too-frequent loſs of life, conſequent on captivity; with all the horrors and peſts of a priſon; together with long abſence from, and inability to give aſſiſtance to, their wives and families.

When they go to the Weſt-Indies, in war time, they run the moſt imminent danger of catching and dying of the

Yellow Fever, through their endeavours to avoid being impreſſed; and, when, after a long abſence from their families, and continuance abroad, they have juſt arrived in view of their homes, they are liable to become, and frequently are, impreſſed into ſhips of war, and therein detained for a ſeries of time, upon much ſlenderer pay, and without the poſſibility of ſeeing their wives and families: all which, none but thoſe who have experienced them, can ſufficiently feel the hardſhip and ſeverity of.

In war time, wearing-apparel and all the neceſſaries of life are much dearer than during peace, which makes a larger ſum of money requiſite for their equipment for ſea and the maintenance of their families.

MERCHANTS and ſhip-owners, alſo, are much better paid for conveying articles of merchandize to and fro, during war, than in peace, on which and the preceding accounts, ſeamen ſhould, I conceive, be conſiderably better paid for their ſervices, in Weſt-India merchantmen, during war than peace, though, perhaps, not to that exorbitant extent they are at preſent in the Weſt-Indies: five pounds per month to thorough able ſeamen, having wives and children, would, perhaps, at this time, contribute to all their reaſonable wants, as well as be a ſufficient remuneration for their ſervices, and at the ſame time allow merchants and ſhip-owners to profecute their commercial concerns to a proper advantage; feamen of the like rank engaged in the Weft-Indies, where neceffaries for a voyage are much dearer than in England, might require feven pounds per month; and fo in proportion to their leffer degrees of ability or ufefulnefs.

SEAMEN, it is alfo neceffary to confider, are, in general, exceffively improvident, and were they to gain ever fo great a fum of money on a voyage, there are few of them that would do otherwife than ftay on-fhore until it was all fpent, and that chiefly in drunkennefs, and other ways that are not only a difgrace to them, but, likewife, detrimental to their health and conftitutions and injurious to their families;

all which muſt ultimately be felt by the ſtate at large, by abating our ſeamen's vigour and courage, and by increaſing the number of indigent and diſtreſſed ſeamen's families.

If ſeamen were more conſiderate, provident, and careful of themſelves, they would, I am certain, from what I have obſerved of them, and of human nature in general, be leſs courageous and adventurous in their country's ſervice and defence: ſurely, then, it is both juſt and requiſite, that this, their peculiar frame of mind, from which the country derives ſuch manifold advantages, ſhould be corrected and reſtrained from proving hurtful to them or their families; and this might, I conceive, eaſily be effected, by making a more adequate and permanent reſerve than is done at preſent, out of their wages and prize-money, for their wants in infirm old age, for the diſablements they are liable to through diſeaſes and accidents, and for the ſupport of their families.

WHOEVER has ſeen the comfortable and even reſpectable proviſion, that is made at Greenwich hoſpital, for old, infirm, and diſabled, ſeamen, of the royal navy, if he poſſeſs the leaſt drop of the " milk of human kindneſs," ſo charmingly and benevolently deſcribed by Shakſpear, muſt, I am ſure, lament that there is not a ſimilar retirement and aſylum for thoſe that ſerve, and are neceſſary to the proſperity of, the merchant: the great wages they get, during both peace and war, beyond thoſe ſerving in the royal navy, and their prize-money, no part of which it is in their nature to make a proper uſe of, together with the known benevolence of the nation, and its intereſt in the welfare and encouragement of ſeamen, would afford an ample fund and ſcope for the eſtabliſhment of ſuch a deſirable inſtitution.

THE making a more adequate, as well as a more permanent, reſerve and proviſion, out of the wages of ſeamen, for the maintenance of their families, would, perhaps, in the end, prove a very great national benefit, by inducing young women of the lower order more frequently to marry ſeamen, and ſeamen the oftener to get married: ſeamen would, confequently, lead more fober and virtuous lives, and beget children, which they rarely do now, at leaft, not to that extent that they ought, and might be expected, from the greatnefs of their numbers; and then, like landfmen, they would have an offspring to bring up, with peculiar pride and pleafure to themfelves, and alfo with advantage to the ftate, in the practice and habits of their own profeffion: this mode of increafing our feamen, might be ftill farther improved, by a gratuity to every feaman, his wife, or his child fo trained up to ferve his country.

Providing in this manner for the wives and infant children of feamen, would, alfo, tend greatly to leffen the poor's rates in thoſe pariſhes where ſeamen's wives and families live.

THE commanders of merchantmen, alſo ſhould be reſtrained from giving to one ſeaman more wages than to another, for, unleſs that is done, it will be to little purpoſe regulating ſeamen's demands, they will, as before, be ever diſſatisfied, unſettled in their minds, and on the look-out for ſhips and captains who are in the greateſt want of men, and will ſecretly give them more money than others, which captains of ſhips are very apt to do, and which contributes greatly to raiſe and keep up the demands and expectations of ſeamen.

SEAMEN ſhould, likewiſe, be reſtrained and bound by articles, under ſome pain or penalty, or the forfeiture of their wages and certain privileges, not to leave their ſhips in the Weſt-Indies, which they are very apt to do, on every trifling occaſion of fancy or diſlike: this might be farther effectuated by not ſuffering any ſeaman to engage himſelf, nor any captain to engage a ſeaman, in the Weſt Indies, unleſs ſuch ſeaman produce a certificate of a regular diſcharge from the captain he laſt ſerved.

THESE things being done would, it is preſumed, very juſtly, liberally, and advantageouſly, for all parties, moſt effectually prevent ſeamen deſerting, from both ſhips of war and merchantmen, for the ſake of exorbitant wages, as well as on all other improper occaſions, and thereby prove the means of preſerving them greatly from the Yellow Fever.

REMARK.

SEVERAL days after this part of my taſk was completed, it came to my knowledge that an Act of Parliament had very lately paſſed, to regulate Weſt-India merchants' ſeamen's wages, and to prevent their deſertion from one ſhip to another in the Weſt-Indies, which, moſt happily, does away all the loſs and ſufferings of ſeamen, I have repreſented to reſult from the heretofore want of ſuch regulation; but, it yet remains to incline ſeamen to ſpend the fruits of their labour to the beſt advantage to themſelves, to their families, and to their country, which, it is earneſtly hoped, will alſo ſoon be undertaken by the ſame illuſtrious perſonages.

THE little time I had to tarry on-ſhore, when the Act of Parliament came to my hands. would not allow me to abridge my work, of this, now, unneceſſary part, it being, as the reader muſt ſee, ſo intimately connected with other parts of my ſubject, and of ſuch magnitude and force, as to the loſs of ſeamen I had undertaken, and nearly completed, the demonſtration of, that it could not be detached therefrom, without entirely altering the plan I had previouſly formed, which time would not allow.

I was, therefore, neceſſitated to ſubmit my work to the preſs, as it was originally framed : this part of it may, perhaps, prove ſatisfactory to the inquiſitive, and ſtand as a memorial of the evil which has been removed, by the late wiſe and timely interference of Parliament. It will, alſo, ſhew how extenſively I have had my country and my fellow creatures benefit in view; and ſerve as a leſſon of humility, to thoſe who pretend to vaſt diſcoveries, which, like mine, may be, at the ſame time, in embryo, in the minds of many other perſons, as well as actually coming forth in various parts.

SECTION THE SECOND.

Suggeſtions for the abolition of the impreſs ſervice, on the Weſt-India ſtation, and for preventing merchant's ſeamen leaving their ſhips, and going on-ſhore, in the Weſt-Indies, to avoid being impreſſed, in order to their preſervation from the Yellow Fever.

THIS is ſurely a moſt important and delicate part of the ſubject under conſideration, and I ſhall beg leave to recapitulate the many injurious and fatal conſequences, which I have ſhewn to reſult from the impreſs ſervice, on the

Weſt India ſtation, in order more ſeriouſly to engage the attention of thoſe who have the power either to aboliſh or ameliorate them.

The impreſs ſervice, in the firſt place, militates againſt the native and conſtitutional freedom of the ſeamen, and ſubjects them, as I have ſhewn, in their endeavours to preſerve that rightful liberty, as well as thoſe employed to deprive them of it, to a moſt rapacious diſeaſe, the Yellow Fever, the extenſive ravages of which, in conſequence, and among both, as I have alſo ſhewn, are ſuch as humanity muſt ſhudder at, and at times render the ſhips of war not only very little better, but even worſe, for having had recourſe to ſuch oppreſſive means to obtain ſeamen.

SHIPS of war on the Weſt-India ſtation, it is to be lamented, have not, at preſent, any other way of being recruited with ſeamen than impreſſing, after the manner I have deſcribed, thoſe that are brought therein by the merchantmen, which cauſes conſiderable interruption to the buſineſs of the merchantmen, in the Weſt-Indies, and is, not unfrequently, practiſed to ſuch extent, as not only to leave them to be entirely unloaded, as well as reloaded, at a very great expence, by negroes, but ſometimes even oblige them to put to ſea, and be navigated home, with infinite riſk and diſtreſs, by half, and at times even not more than a third of, their wonted and requiſite number of people.

IMPRESSING ſeamen from the merchantmen is, alſo, one of the chief cauſes of that ſcarcity and want of ſeamen, at the departure of large fleets of merchantmen from the Weſt-Indies, which obliges the captains thereof to give the enormous ſums of money I have repreſented to ſeamen, for barely working their ſhips home, and which induces ſeamen, at the great peril of their lives, to deſert from one merchantman to another, and even from ſhips of war.

THE accommodation of all perſons, and of both merchantmen and ſhips of war, as well as the prevention of the loſs of ſeamen, through the impreſs ſervice, ſurely demands the moſt ſerious attention, and I ſhall accordingly prefume to fhew how I humbly conceive the whole may be accomplifhed, hoping that if my fuggefting fhould appear futile, they will, notwithftanding, be the means of exciting the attention of perfons better qualified to treat on the fubject, and of bringing forth, from abler heads and pens, more eligible propofitions.

I. I humbly propofe that Weft-India merchantmen have two apprentices for each hundred tons of their burthen, to be bound for the term of three or five years, which, if they were properly encouraged and put forward, and not taken at too early an age, would be a fufficient time for them to be made at leaft exceedingly ferviceable, if not tolerably good, ſeamen. The merchants' ſervice would thus become a vaſt nurſery for ſeamen, and, ſuppoſing the aggregate of the tonnage of the ſeveral deſcriptions of merchantmen, which I have ſaid go annually to the Weſt-Indies, to be three hundred thouſand,* then every three or five years would produce and put forth ſix thouſand ſeamen. Theſe ſix thouſand apprentices, would, beſides, take the places of ſo many able ſeamen and landſmen, who are now, of neceſſity, employed in the merchants' ſervice, and who, conſequently, for the moſt part, would be led and obliged to enter into the royal navy; and ſuch as did not enter would,

* This eſtimate is taken from Mr. Bailie's ſpeech on the abolition of the ſlave-trade, April 2, 1792.

moſt probably, become impreſſed, whereby ſix thouſand ſeamen would be added to the ſtrength and ſervice of the royal navy: the merchantmen would thereby, alſo, have conſtantly ſome aſſiſtance throughout their voyages, and never be entirely without hands, as they now too frequently are, in the Weſt-Indies, through deſertion as well as impreſſing.

II. That merchants' ſhips employ ſeamen of foreign nations in amity with us, in the number and proportion of one for every hundred tons of their burthen, which would, likewiſe, be of farther conſiderable advantage to the royal navy, by their occupying the places of ſo many Britiſh ſeamen, who muſt otherwiſe be employed in the merchants' ſervice. At the time of engaging foreign ſeamen, the commanders of merchantmen ſhould ſee, and take eſpecial care, that they have proper certificates, from their reſpective conſuls, to ſhew that they really are foreigners and to protect them from being impreſſed; through neglect of which, they are liable to be, and I have often ſeen them, very unexpectedly to themſelves and the captains of merchantmen, impreſſed in common with Britiſh ſeamen. Theſe foreign ſeamen I propoſe to be called, and conſidered as, part of merchantmen's ſtanding complements.

III. THAT merchants' ſhips employ,

for each hundred tons of their burthen, one ſeaman at a certain advanced age, ſay forty or fifty years, or that had ſerved ſuch a length of time in the royal navy, as 15, 20, 25, or 30, years: ſuch men would be, I conceive, particularly neceſſary and ſerviceable towards inſtructing and training up the apprentices; and it would, perhaps, greatly encourage ſeamen to enter into, and not deſert from, the ſervice of the royal navy, were they to be exempted from ſerving therein, unleſs they choſe it, alſo, from being impreſſed out of merchantmen, at and after any of the ſaid ages and terms of ſervitude. Theſe people I would, alſo, have made part of merchantmen's ſtanding complements.

IV. There are many ſeamen, and likewiſe landſmen, who, after having ſuffered amputation of their legs, in private hoſpitals, and their ſtumps being got quite well, know not how to ſupport themſelves, nor, as I lately ſaw two inſtances at the London-Hoſpital, whither to go, not even for a night's lodging: there are, alſo, ſeamen who ſuffer amputation on board ſhips of war, and in naval hoſpitals, whoſe ſmart-money, as it is called, or penſion, not being adequate to their ſupport, are often reduced to a ſimilar ſituation as the former deſcription of men. It really would be the greateſt humanity, were merchants, and captains of merchantmen, to ſeek for and employ all ſuch perſons conſtantly in their ſhips; they would be able to do the duty of cooks, and when in harbour that of ſhip-keepers, very well, and ſuch men are, at all times and places, exempt from being impreſſed: I have had one ſuch perſon under my direction, as a cook, on a ſlaving-voyage: his duty was arduous, and. yet, he performed it very well. The number of theſe people would, altogether, be too inconſiderable to form a part, or even make one, of every merchant-ſhip's complement, they would, however, ſupply the places of many able-bodied men, who, in conſequence, would become employed to much greater advantage in other ſtations, on-board both merchantmen and ſhips of war.

V. THAT merchant-ſhips be allowed two able Britiſh ſeamen for each hundred tons of their burthen, two of which, in each ſhip, to rank as chief and ſecond mates, and to be conſidered as part of her ſtanding complement, the reſt as ſupernumeraries: except in veſſels of only one hundred tons burthen, in which the captains commonly doing the duty of an officer, when at ſea, the ſecond mate ſhould be conſidered as a ſupernumerary.

VI. THAT merchant-ſhips be allowed two able landſmen for each hundred tons of their burthen, one of them, in each ſhip, to be a carpenter and conſidered as part of her ſtanding complement, the reſt as ſupernumeraries:

this would give young landſmen, of roving and enterpriſing diſpoſitions, an opportunity to go to ſea; alſo, for tradeſmen and mechanics out of employ to get bread, which would farther make the merchants' ſervice a nurſery for ſeamen.

COROLLARY I.

According to the foregoing propoſitions, each merchantman of one hundred tons burthen would have eight people, ſix of them her ſtanding complement and two of them ſupernumeraries; thoſe of two hundred tons would have ſixteen people, eleven of them her ſtanding complement and five ſupernumeraries; thoſe of three hundred tons would have twenty-four people, fifteen of them her ſtanding complement and nine of them ſupernumeraries; thoſe of four hundred tons would have thirty-two people, nineteen of them her ſtanding complement and thirteen of them ſupernumeraries; thoſe of five hundred tons would have forty people, twenty-three of them her ſtanding complement and ſeventeen of them ſupernumeraries; and merchantmen of ſix hundred tons burthen, which are nearly the largeſt employed in the trade, would have forty-eight people, twenty-ſeven of them her ſtanding complement and twenty-one ſupernumeraries; which number and proportion of people would be fully ſufficient for them to be reſpectively navigated to the Weſt-Indies, and rather more than would be required to unload and reload them after their arrival in the Weſt-Indies.

VII. The African ſlave-ſhips, which, as I before noted, are in the proportion of about one to three of the properly called Weſt-Indiamen, or ſugar-ſhips, would on the ſlaving part of their voyages require double the ſaid number and proportion of men, the neceſſity for which would be done away on their arrival in the Weſt-Indies; and which additional people I propoſe for them to have, and be allowed, according to their owners' and commanders' liking and conveniency; and to be conſidered as ſupernumeraries.

VIII. In order to recruit the complements of ſhips of war on the Weſt-India ſtation, in the next place, I would propoſe, that each ſugar-ſhip of one hundred tons burthen be required, on her arrival in the Weſt-Indies, to turn over to a ſhip of war one of her ſupernumeraries; thoſe of two hundred tons, two; thoſe of three hundred tons, four; thoſe of four hundred tons, ſix; thoſe of five hundred tons, eight; and each of thoſe of ſix hundred tons burthen to turn over ten of her ſupernumeraries.

IX. THE African ſlave-ſhips bury, upon an average, it may be computed, at leaſt a fourth of their people, by the time they arrive in the Weſt-Indies, and have often ſeveral in a very ſickly ſtate; I, therefore, propoſe, on their arrival in the Weſt-Indies, filling up the vacancies in their ſtanding complements, from their ſupernumeraries, and then, if ſickneſs did not prevent, that each ſhip of one hundred tons burthen be required to turn over to a ſhip of war two of her ſupernumeraries; thoſe of two hundred tons, ſix; thoſe of three hundred tons, ten; and thoſe of four hundred tons burthen, which are the largeſt in the trade, to turn over fourteen of their ſupernumeraries.

X. THE offer and ſake of his majeſty's bounty, would frequently induce the ſupernumeraries to enter voluntarily into the ſervice of the ſhips of war, in the number and proportions I have propoſed; but, when it did not, I propoſe, that the whole of the ſupernumeraries in each ſhip draw lots who ſhall, in the ſaid number and proportions, be turned over to, and ſerve in, the ſhips of war: in the latter way, all the ſupernumeraries would have hopes, and a chance alike, of not being ſelected for the ſervice of the ſhips of war, which would induce them to ſtay on-board and take their chance, in common with each other, and not leave their ſhips, as I have ſhewn they do now, at the riſk of their lives, to ſcreen and hide themſelves on-ſhore.

This mode of procuring and obliging ſeamen to ſerve in the royal navy would be, alſo, I conceive, perfectly conſtitutional, inaſmuch as perſons of almoſt every deſcription, throughout the land, are by law required, and ſubmit to the chance of being ſelected and drawn by lot, to ſerve their country as militia-men; why, then, ſhould not ſeafaring men, in the merchants' ſervice, be required to ſerve their country, in the like manner, by ſea? it ſurely would be infinitely more equitable, as well as conſiderably leſs oppreſſive, than the preſent practice of impreſſing and taking them by force: I have, in truth, known them to accede to it with the utmoſt readineſs, which makes me preſume to propoſe it, and inclines me to believe it would be highly ſatisfactory to ſeafaring men in general.

COROLLARY II.

Ships of war on the Weſt-India ſtation would, by the means I have propofed, receive from the fugar and African flave fhips, taken little and great together, at leaft two men for each hundred tons of their burthen, which, agreeably to the before-faid aggregate of their tonnage, would amount to fix thoufand men annually.

COROLLARY III.

After the faid drafts of men into the fhips of war, fugar-fhips of one hundred tons burthen would have feven people belonging to them; thofe of two hundred tons would have fourteen people, three of them fupernumeraries; thofe of three hundred tons would have twenty people, five of them fupernumeraries; thofe of four hundred tons would have twenty-ſix people, ſeven of them ſupernumeraries; thoſe of five hundred tons would have thirty-two people, nine of them ſupernumeraries; and thoſe of ſix hundred tons burthen would have thirty-eight people, eleven of them ſupernumeraries: the African ſlave-ſhips, of one hundred tons burthen, would have ten people, three of them ſupernumeraries; thoſe of two hundred tons would have eighteen people, ſeven of them ſupernumeraries; thoſe of three hundred tons would have twenty-ſix people, eleven of them ſupernumeraries; and thoſe of four hundred tons burthen would have thirty-four people, fifteen of them ſupernumeraries; which number and proportion of people would be, as I am informed, fully ſufficient for them to be reſpectively unloaded, reloaded, and navigated home.

XI. In caſe the before-ſaid annual recruit of ſix thouſand men, ſhould not, on particular times and occaſions, prove ſufficient for the ſhips of war on the Weſt India ſtation, I farther propoſe that ſugar-ſhips of two hundred tons burthen ſhould, in the before-ſaid manner, turn over to a ſhip of war two more of their ſupernumeraries; thoſe of three hundred tons, three; thoſe of four hundred tons, four; thoſe of five hundred tons, five; and thoſe of ſix hundred tons burthen to turn over ſix of their ſupernumeraries: the African ſlave-ſhips, alſo, in the like manner, of one hundred tons burthen, to turn over to a ſhip of war one more of their ſupernumeraries; thoſe of two huudred tons, three; thoſe of three hundred tons, four; and thoſe of four hundred tons burthen to turn over five more of their ſupernumeraries.

COROLLARY IV.

THE ſhips of war on the Weſt-India ſtation would receive, by the laſt propoſition, from the ſugar and African ſlave ſhips, taken little and great together, at leaſt one man for each hundred tons of their burthen, which, according to the aggregate of their tonnage, would annually amount to three thouſand men, which, with the former ſupply of ſix thouſand, makes nine thouſand men annually, which is, I conceive, nearly, if not more than, twice as many, as they now receive by the more harſh, oppreſſive, and fatal, mode of impreſſing them, and which, I farther preſume to conceive, would greatly exceed the demand that the ſhips of war on the Weſt-India ſtation could at any time have for ſeamen: they would, alſo, be obtained with much leſs trouble and without ſubjecting their people to the cauſes of the Yellow Fever.

COROLLARY V.

AFTER the ſecond draft of men from the merchantmen, ſugar-ſhips of one hundred tons burthen would have ſeven people belonging to them; thoſe of two hundred tons would have twelve; thoſe of three hundred tons would have ſeventeen; thoſe of four hundred tons would have twenty-two; thoſe of five hundred tons would have twenty-ſeven; and thoſe of ſix hundred tons burthen would have thirty-two people belonging to them: the African ſlave-ſhips of one hundred tons burthen would have nine people; thoſe of two hundred tons would have fifteen; thoſe of three hundred tons would have twenty-two; and thoſe of four hundred tons burthen would have twenty-nine people belonging to them; which number and proportion of people, if not found ſufficient to do their buſineſs in the Weſt-Indies, nor to navigate them home, I would propoſe the following expedients.

XII. That they hire negroes while in the Weſt-Indies; whoſe labour, when hired by the week or month, would, I conceive, be obtained as cheaply, if not more ſo, than that of ſeamen in war time.

XIII. That, when loaded and ready to ſail, they be allowed, and each take, as want aſſiſtance, a few priſoners of war, who would, I know, from much obſervation, very gladly work, and do any thing but fight againſt their country, for the ſake of being releaſed from a loathſome priſon, a belly full of victuals, and a little money to buy clothes; which it would be well worth the merchants' while to give them; and which would greatly relieve the people of the Weſt-India iſlands from the expence of maintaining them, as well as favor their return to, and exchange in, France, or whatever other nation they might be natives of. The fleet of merchantmen I came home in company with, from Jamaica, in June, 1796, employed a great many French priſoners of war; and they were in general paid moſt extravagantly for merely their ſervices on the paſſage; the ſhip I belonged to, the P-l-g--m, as before noted, employed four, one of them had forty guineas, and the other three had fifty guineas each, for only aſſiſting to work the ſhip home.

XIV. Should the preceding claſs of propoſitions be thought too complex and troubleſome, I farther preſume to ſubmit for conſideration, that the merchantmen be allowed to have, exempt from being impreſſed, a ſufficient number of men to navigate them and do their buſineſs in the Weſt-Indies, in quality either ſuch as has been propoſed, or as otherwiſe may be thought more eligible; and, that the ſhips of war on the Weſt-India ſtation be recruited with ſeamen, by occaſionally ſending ſhips of war to them from England, with a proper number of ſupernumeraries.

GENERAL INFERENCE.

Either claſs of the foregoing propoſitions, if adopted, would, it is preſumed, with great fairneſs to the ſeamen, and advantage to both merchantmen and ſhips of war, entirely aboliſh and do away the neceſſity for the impreſs ſervice in the Weſt-Indies; whereby the loſs of ſeamen, by the Yellow Fever, which I have repreſented to happen in conſequence of ſeamen leaving merchantmen, in the Weſt-Indies, and going on-ſhore, to avoid being impreſſed, would be moſt effectually prevented.

If, however, it ſhould be thought more eligible and proper for the Weſt-India merchantmen to be manned, and for the impreſſing of ſeamen from them in the Weſt-Indies to be continued, as heretofore, then, agreeably to the other head of this ſection, I propoſe, in order to ſave ſeamen's lives, which I hope will be taken in excuſe for my propoſing ſuch arbitrary meaſures as

I. THAT captains of Weſt-India merchantmen, of every deſcription, be reſtrained and bound, under ſome pain or penalty, not to ſuffer nor encourage their people to leave their ſhips, and go on-ſhore, to avoid being impreſſed; and to be obligated to muſter, if poſſible, the whole of their people brought into the Weſt-Indies, before the firſt ſhip of war's officer that boards them.

IT is common for the commanders of merchantmen, at all times, but particularly on their firſt arrival in the Weſt-Indies, and before they get ſo near to a harbour as to be boarded by boats from the ſhips of war, to let a part of their crew take a boat and go on-ſhore, or elſe, to hide in various parts of the ſhip, in order to ſave them from being impreſſed, in the firſt inſtance: ſome are, almoſt always, taken, either on-board or on-ſhore, and they, through vexation, often inform on the reſt; a ſtrict look-out on the ſhip is, in conſequence for ſome time after kept, by the ſhips of war boats, till, by frequent ſurprizals, the greateſt part of the people are often in the end taken; and thoſe that are not, rarely have ſufficient gratitude to continue with the captains, who ſo preſerved them from being impreſſed, any longer than till they find a better paymaſter or a ſhip more to their fancy: the trouble, the vexation, the interruption to buſineſs, and the frequent inutility of thoſe artifices, and above all the great injury thereby done to the health and lives of ſeamen, ſhould induce the captains of merchantmen to diſcontinue the practice of them, if not, they might, as I propoſed, be bound and reſtrained therefrom, under ſome pain or penalty.

II. To puniſh and reſtrain the practices of a ſet of men, called landlords and crimps, who encourage ſeamen to deſert from both ſhips of war and merchantmen, provide them with hiding-places, and encourage them in their enormous demands for wages, in order that they may keep them the longer with them, and charge them the more extravagantly; and after all recommend, or rather ſell and diſpoſe of, them, to ſuch captains as offer moſt money for procuring ſeamen.

SECTION THE THIRD.

General means of preſerving ſeamen from the Yellow Fever, during the loading and continuance of merchantmen in the Weſt-Indies, and when they muſt of neceſſity go on-ſhore, on their ſhip's duty or for their own recreation. Alſo, the proper place that ſhould be allowed them to ſleep in.

COMMANDERS of merchantmen will ſurely, by this time, clearly underſtand and be convinced that the grand and only means of preſerving their ſeamen from the Yellow Fever, are, to keep them without the influence of the effluvia, generated, in warm climates, from putrid animal and vegetable ſubſtances; alſo, to a ſober conduct, and regular performance of duty, on-board their ſhips.

To effect the former, they ſhould moor their ſhips, on their arrival in the Weſt-Indies, as far from the ſhore as their buſineſs will admit, but, particularly, from low marſhy lands, ſavannas, and ſtagnant waters; they ſhould, likewiſe, berth their ſhips where they will be the leaſt land-locked or expoſed to the land wind, and the moſt open to the ſea and ſea breeze: unfortunately, ſuch choice is not to be made in many parts, but when, and as far as, it is practicable, ſhould be moſt religiouſly attended to.

SEAMEN might be kept on-board, and greatly preſerved from the Yellow Fever, by employing a few negroes, to go in boats to fetch the cargo and water, from parts ſo far diſtant, as require to be away one, two, or more, nights and days, alſo, when the captain and other officers require to be taken to or from the ſhore, after ſun-ſet: negroes, as I before obſerved, can be made to work more ſteadily than ſeamen, many of them are, alſo, much more uſeful in droghing for ſugars and ſtowing a ſhip's hold, and are not ſo ſuſceptible of the Yellow Fever, when expoſed in boats: when, likewiſe, they are hired by the week or month, their labour would, I conceive, be obtained as cheaply, if not more ſo in the end, than that of ſeamen, during war.

WHERE negroes are not to be obtained, the ſeamen might be greatly preſerved, in the boating duty, by providing them with good huts to ſhelter and ſleep in, at the different wharfs and cranes where they go to deliver or receive a loading; alſo, by employing as large boats as conveniently may be, with a ſhort deck or cuddy forward, for them to ſhelter and ſleep in; and, when they muſt of neceſſity continue all night, in ſmall open boats, by providing them with good great or watch coats, and tarpaulings, to guard them from the rain, and the peſtilential and fatal influence of the dews and night-air.

Where the diſtances to and from places, to which boats are employed, are ſo ſhort, and the winds and tides ſo favorable, that a trip can be made within twelve hours, the boatmen ſhould be ſent away at ſun-riſe, that they may be back before ſun-ſet and the falling of the dew: for want of ſuch management, I have often ſeen ſeamen unneceſſarily expoſed by night, and thereby brought into danger, and even within the graſp of death.

Persons exhauſted by both hunger and fatigue, in the Weſt-Indies, are then very ſuſceptible of the Yellow Fever: when, therefore, ſeamen are required to go in boats, to ſuch diſtances from the ſhip as will oblige them to be abſent during one or more meals, they ſhould be ſupplied with a proper quantity of ready-dreſſed proviſions, and a moderate allowance of ſpirits, for the time they are likely to be abſent.

HARD labour, in the Weſt-Indies, and its attendant, exceſſive ſweating, by day, very much diſpoſes the body to receive hurtful impreſſions from the night-air, which commanders of merchantmen ſhould, in humanity and juſtice, both on their buſineſs and pleaſures, conſider, and preſerve their ſeamen from, by either going on-ſhore and returning on-board before ſun-ſet, or by employing negroes and ſhore-boats, on ſuch occaſions, by night, and not keep ſeamen, after the fatigues of the day, waiting for them, and ſleeping, at the riſk of their lives, in open boats, as they often do. I have frequently ſeen them, till very late hours, and even ſun-riſe.

Recreation, is what every man, at times, requires, and ought to have, or life would be irkſome, particularly to ſeamen, who ſpend many weeks at a time on the wide and dreary main: ſeamen ſhould, therefore, be allowed to go on-ſhore, in the Weſt-Indies, by turns, on Sundays, but they ſhould not be ſuffered to ſtay after ſun-ſet nor all night, as expoſure to the night-air, and drinking hard for any length of time, in the Weſt-Indies, which ſailors always do, whenever they have opportunity, is ſure to be productive of the Yellow Fever.

It is abſolutely neceſſary towards preſerving the health of ſeamen, and giving them a fair chance of recovering when ſick, in all countries as well as the Weſt-Indies, that they be allowed a proper place to ſleep in, and to ſhelter themſelves in occaſionally from the inclemencies of the weather.

In cold countries, and when at ſea, they ſhould be berthed between decks, and the place allotted them ſhould have two or more air-ports in it; alſo, cloſe bulk-heads to preclude the offenſive ſteam that ariſes from ſugars: in the Weſt-Indies, the beſt, and I ſhould imagine, while ſhips are loading there, the moſt convenient, places for the ſeamen to be lodged in, are under the half-deck or forecaſtle, with canvaſs ſcreens at the open parts, to prevent the ingreſs of the night-air and rain; or, in ſhips not frigate-built, a ſmall wooden awning or round-about houſe, might, I conceive, without any detriment, be erected for that purpoſe, at either the fore or after part of the main-maſt, which I have ſeen done on-board ſome ſhips.

Whichever of theſe different places be appropriated to the uſe of the ſeamen, it ſhould not be incumbered with any part of the ſhip's cargo or ſtores, or lumber of any kind; and there ſhould be room enough allowed for conveniently ſlinging hammocks, for at leaſt half the ſhip's company; it ſhould, alſo, frequently be either waſhed or ſcraped and fumigated; and be every two or three months lime-whitened, or once in ſix months freſh painted and occaſionally waſhed clean. The ſeamen's hammocks, likewiſe, ſhould be, at leaſt every month or two, ſcrubbed clean, and every fine day taken above deck and expoſed to the air and ſun.

In theſe ſeveral ways ſeamen might be comfortably and properly berthed, without deducting much from the freight; and by being thus kept quite apart from the ſhip's cargo and ſtores, they would be more effectually prevented from any embezzlement of them, which I have frequently heard great complaints about, and which their preſent improper manner of being lodged affords them many opportunities of doing.

SECTION THE FOURTH.

Means of providing, in the ſpeedieſt manner, medical and ſurgical aſſiſtance, and other requiſite help, for Weſt-India merchants' ſeamen, when they are ſick and have received accidents.

I Have, I truſt, very ſufficiently ſhewn that ſeamen, in the Weſt-India merchants' ſervice, do not, at preſent, get ſuch ſpeedy and effectual medical and ſurgical aſſiſtance, nor other neceſſary help, when they are ſick and hurt, as is not only needful but, likewiſe, as humanity, juſtice, and national policy, require they ſhould have.

In order to ſuch highly requiſite aſſiſtance being given to ſeamen, every merchant-ſhip, without exception, ſhould be required to employ a ſurgeon; and, in caſe it ſhould not be found practicable to obtain a ſufficient number at once, the moſt proper ſhips to be exempted, for the preſent, are ſuch as do not ſail armed and that carry the feweſt men.

For the relief of the ſeamen of thoſe veſſels that could not get ſurgeons, I would propoſe that the ſurgeons be ſo appointed to, and diſtributed among, the Weſt-Indiamen, as that every port in the Weſt-Indies, alſo, every loading-place, where aſſiſtance could not readily be obtained from ſhore, ſhould, according to the number of veſſels that commonly reſorted to them, have one, two, or more ſurgeons to be in them every loading-ſeaſon, and, if practicable, at all times; and, that the ſurgeons be allowed, engaged, and ſent for as often as requiſite, to give aſſiſtance to the ſeamen of ſhips not having ſurgeons on-board, and provided with a boat for the purpoſe, on all neceſſary occaſions.

It is here again neceſſary to obſerve, that the Yellow Fever is one of the moſt deceiving and fatal diſeaſes to which mankind is ſubject; it often commences with very ſlight complaints and terminates life in a very few hours, and very little neglect of time on the part of a ſeaman in applying for medical aſſiſtance, or on the ſide of the captain in procuring him that help, may be the occaſion of attacks, that would not otherwiſe have terminated unfavorably, proceeding to a dangerous and even incurable height; and farther, unleſs the phyſician is called early, attends regularly, and has his medicines faithfully adminiſtered, little will his viſits avail: on the contrary, by early and proper attention, a very great proportion of perſons affected by the Yellow Fever, may be reſtored to health, in a ſhort time, and be recovered from even very violent and dangerous attacks.

It ſhould, alſo, be particularly obſerved, that ſeamen are, in general, very backward in acquainting their commanders, ſuperior officers, and even ſurgeons of ſhips, with their ailments; and many of them, through the hopes of their diſorders ſoon wearing off, or from pride, bravado, a ſulky or a moroſe temper, will, eſpecially when influenced by a little grog, continue to perform their duty, for a long time, and ſtruggle with their complaints until they acquire a very great degree of violence; whereby, through the mere neglect of timely application, they often bring themſelves into the moſt imminent danger, and even paſt recovery.

THEREFORE, it behoves all commanders and commanding officers of Weſt-Indiamen, not having ſurgeons on-board, not only to pay immediate attention to the ſlighteſt complaint of indiſpoſition from a ſeaman, but, likewiſe, when any of them appear ſickly, or abate of their wonted alacrity and cheerfulneſs, to queſtion them as to the cauſe, and whenever medical help is required, to delay no time in obtaining it for them, from either a ſhip in company or the ſhore.

WHEN it ſo happened that ſeamen were taken ſick of the Yellow Fever, in any harbour in the Weſt-Indies, and there was not a ſhip in company having a ſurgeon on-board to give them immediate aſſiſtance, nor one that could be ſpeedily obtained from the ſhore; or, in caſe there was ſuch help at hand, but no one could poſſibly be ſpared to attend them, nor a proper place provided for them to ſleep in, they ſhould, under all ſuch circumſtances, be taken, without delay, on ſhore, and placed in a houſe where they would have proper medical and ſurgical aſſiſtance, alſo, other requiſite attendance and help of every kind, and be under proper controul: the Yellow Fever, it has been obſerved, is almoſt the only diſeaſe that affects ſeamen in the Weſt-Indies, and it ſoon runs its courſe, terminating either in health or death in a few days, and often indeed in a few hours; ſo that a trifling expence would ſuffice.

THE naval and military hoſpitals, where ſuch are, would be very proper places to remove ſick ſeamen into, and the terms of admiſſion would, perhaps, be eaſier than in private houſes. All extraordinary bad caſes, and accidents, requiring particular judgement or length of time, or any capital operation, ſhould alſo, have ready admiſſion into ſuch hoſpitals.

BEFORE ſurgeons are engaged in Weſt-Indiamen, they ſhould have their qualifications proved by a proper examination, before able perſons, duly appointed for the purpoſe, in the different ſea-ports to which the merchant-ſhips belonged: and their pay, emoluments, treatment, and accommodations, ſhould be ſuch, as would make it both worth while and agreeable to young men qualified to undergo ſuch an examination, and to give the relief required, to enter into the merchants' ſervice. To effect theſe very deſirable objects, the ſurgeon's wages ſhouid not, I conceive, at theſe times, be leſs than five guineas per month ; they, alſo, ſhould be provided with medicines and inſtruments at the owner's expence, or, what would perhaps be better for all parties, allowed a proper ſum of money to ſupply thoſe neceſſaries themſelves ; and, when they attended the ſick on-board other ſhips, they ſhould be paid the ſame, or nearly ſo, as ſurgeons employed from the ſhore. They ſhould, likewiſe, meſs with the captain, and be accommodated with a ſmall cabin or ſtate-room, to retire to and ſleep in, alſo, be treated as the friend and companion of the captain, and not required to do any menial offices, as ſurgeons too commonly are in merchantmen.

THERE are, I conceive, many young men, very well qualified to ſerve as ſurgeons of Weſt-Indiamen, who are now obliged to ſacrifice their time and their talents, behind apothecaries' counters, and in other ſituations of no greater profit, and who, on the terms I have mentioned, alſo for the ſake of ſeeing the world, and putting a little money in their pockets to forward them in life, would very ſoon, and cheerfully, preſent themſelves to ſerve in Weſt-India merchantmen.

Besides medical and ſurgical aſſiſtance, ſick and hurt ſeamen require, and ſhould be allowed, a boy or a man, to attend upon them and adminiſter their medicines, to cook for them and prepare their drink, to waſh their linen, and keep them clean.

By the above means, the whole of

the merchantmen's ſeamen, when in the Weſt-Indies, and nearly the whole of them while on their paſſages to and from the Weſt-Indies, would have proper and ſpeedy medical and ſurgical aſſiſtance, as well as other neceſſary accommodation, attendance, and help, when ſick and hurt.

The commanders of ſuch merchantmen as did not carry ſurgeons, might be ſafely directed, in many inſtances, to give medical and even ſurgical aid to their ſeamen, when at ſea, and wherever neither a phyſician's nor a ſurgeon's aſſiſtance could be obtained, if ſome perſon, who has had a regular medical education, and proper experience of the Yellow Fever, were encouraged to undertake a reviſal of their medicine-boxes, and compile a proper book of directions.

APPOINTING surgeons to West-India merchantmen, would also, I humbly conceive, prove, in many respects, very advantageous to the West-India merchants, ship-owners, and captains. The surgeons might be required by contract, when sickness did not disallow, to assist the mates in keeping the ship's log-book, and taking an account of the reception and delivery of the cargo: also, the captain, in his accounts and disbursements, copying his letters, and making out his bills of lading, the last of which, when abroad, they are now commonly obliged to pay others for doing: the merchants and ship-owners would, thereby, have a fair and clear set of books and accounts, put into their hands, immediately on their ſhips arrival home, which they now, I believe, frequently have not, and probably would often give not a trifle to obtain.

THE ſurgeons might, alſo, be employed, by the captains of merchantmen, on many little and not ungentlemanly occaſions, on-ſhore, when they were either buſy, or ſick, or had not another officer to ſpare. Captains of merchantmen, by the appointment of ſurgeons to their ſhips, would likewiſe be freed from the great expence of medical and ſurgical aſſiſtance for themſelves abroad, and always have a perſon at hand to adminiſter relief and comfort to them when ſick at ſea; they would, alſo, have a friend and companion to converſe with, and who would contribute to make leiſure time paſs away pleaſantly; and, moreover, a clever genteel ſurgeon would ultimately be a great pecuniary help to them, by inducing paſſengers to engage in their ſhips.

In theſe ſeveral ways, the ſurgeons might be kept fully employed, without being, I conceive, in the leaſt degraded, and amply repay the merchants and ſhip-owners all expences attendant on their appointment, beſides ſaving many hundreds of very valuable lives, and exciting the moſt pleaſing ſenſations in the minds of men of humane, benevolent, and patriotic, diſpoſitions.

West-India merchantmen would thus become a nurſery for ſea-ſurgeons, whofe previous feafoning to the Weft-India climate, and experience of the Yellow Fever, and of other difeafes incident to feamen, would qualify and fit them, in an efpecial manner, to ferve in our navy in the Weft-Indies; and alfo to be contributory to the improvement of the healing art generally; and it would, perhaps, be good and right to give thofe furgeons particular preference and encouragement to ferve in fhips of war on the Weft-India ftation.

ESTABLISHING, in this manner, a nurfery for fea-furgeons, would furely prove highly beneficial to a great maritime nation, that employs and requires fuch a hoft of mariners.

THE SIXTH PART.

MEANS OF PREVENTING AND AMELIORATING THE BEFORE-SAID LOSS AND SUFFERINGS OF SEAMEN ON-BOARD SHIPS OF WAR ON THE WEST-INDIA STATION.

TO accomplifh the very important objects included under this head, the reader will furely acquiefce with me in the neceffity for either recruiting fhips of war on the Weft-India ftation with feamen, by other means than impreffing them on fhore and out of merchantmen, or elfe caufing them to become impreſſed out of the merchantmen immediately on their arrival in the Weſt-Indies; alſo, appointing ſurgeons to ſhips of war on the Weſt-India ſtation, properly experienced in the nature and treatment of the Yellow Fever; and increaſing the emoluments of naval ſurgeons, on the Weſt-India ſtation, ſo as to enable them to provide a ſufficient quantity of the Peruvian Bark for the relief of the ſick of the Yellow Fever.

SECTION THE FIRST.

Of recruiting ſhips of war on the Weſt-India ſtation, with ſeamen, by other means than impreſſing them on-ſhore and out of merchantmen, and of cauſing merchants' ſeamen to become impreſſed out of their ſhips as ſoon as they arrive in the Weſt-Indies, in order to prevent the introduction of the Yellow Fever into ſhips of war, and to preſerve the ſeamen employed on the impreſs ſervice from the Yellow Fever. Alſo, other means neceſſary to the preſervation of the health and lives of ſeamen, on-board ſhips of war on the Weſt-India ſtation.

FOR the means of effecting the two firſt heads of this ſection, I muſt refer the reader back to my ſuggeſtions for the abolition of the impreſs ſervice on the Weſt-India ſtation, and for preventing merchants' ſeamen leaving their ſhips and going on-ſhore, in the Weſt-Indies, to avoid being impreſſed: the former, if adopted, would, it is preſumed, amply recruit the ſhips of war with ſeamen, without either impreſſing or expoſing the ſeamen of ſhips of war to the cauſes of the Yellow Fever; and by the latter means propoſed, the merchants' ſeamen would become impreſſed before being at all expoſed on-ſhore to the cauſes of the Yellow Fever, as alſo, without expoſing the ſeamen employed in impreſſing them to the cauſes of the diſeaſe, whereby the introduction of the Yellow Fever into the ſhips of war on the Weſt-India ſtation, and the loſs of ſeamen by it, on-board ſhips of war, which I have repreſented to happen through the impreſs ſervice, would be moſt effectually prevented.

In addition to the above means of preſerving the health and lives of ſeamen, on-board ſhips of war on the Weſt-India ſtation, I would propoſe, that, occaſionally, there be ſhips of war ſent to the Weſt-Indies, to relieve and take the places of ſuch ſhips whoſe crews are, and have been for any length of time, unuſually ſickly, for it ſometimes happens through the greatneſs of the number of ſeamen ſick of the Yellow Fever, on-board a ſhip at one time, and through the unuſual malignancy of the Fever at particular periods, that it ſpreads, by contagion, to thoſe ſeamen who have been kept conſtantly on-board, and not been in the leaſt ex-poſed to the common cauſes of the Yel-low Fever, till, at length, the diſeaſe runs entirely through the crew, and ſo impairs their conſtitutions, in general, that many of them are conſtantly la-bouring under and dying of relapſes, as well as of firſt attacks, and which will ſometimes continue for ſeveral weeks, and even months, notwithſtand-ing the utmoſt attention to cleanlineſs, and the common preventatives of the Yellow Fever.

Under theſe circumſtances, the effluvia arifing from the bodies of the fick, which, it is well known to medical men, greatly contaminate the air, and, thereby, caufe very malignant fevers, are diffufed throughout the fhip, and even pervade and become pent up within every crevice and vacant place, and thence become a continual fource of ficknefs to frefh comers on-board, and to thofe who have not been expofed to the ufual caufes of ficknefs in the Weft-Indies. Many of the feamen, alfo, who recover from firft attacks of the Yellow Fever, have their conftitutions thereby fo much impaired, that, as long as they continue in the Weft-Indies, they are fubject to frequent and periodical relapfes, like fo many perfons affected with habitual agues.

In ſuch caſe, the moſt ſpeedy and only means indeed, of permanently purifying a ſhip, and reſtoring her crew to health, are to relieve her from her ſtation and order her home; the change of air and climate, as ſoon as ſhe gets to the northward of the Tropic of Cancer, will have an immediate and almoſt miraculous good effect on the health and conſtitutions of the ſeamen; and as ſoon as ſhe arrives in port, all her ſtores and ballaſt ſhould be taken out and expoſed to the air; ſhe ſhould, alſo, be thoroughly ventilated, cleaned, fumigated, and freſh painted, before being engaged in any farther ſervice, more eſpecially in a warm climate.

In order more completely to preſerve the health and lives of ſeamen, in the

Weſt-Indies, I beg leave to recommend to the commanders of ſhips of war, an obſervance of the ſeveral means pointed out in ſection the third, page 202, which will ſave me unneceſſary recapitulation in this part.

SECTION THE SECOND.

Of the neceſſity for appointing, and the means of obtaining, ſurgeons for ſhips of war on the Weſt-India ſtation, properly experienced in the nature and treatment of the Yellow Fever. Alſo, of the education requiſite for a naval ſurgeon.

THE prevalence and fatality of the Yellow Fever among ſeamen in the Weſt-Indies, over and above all other diſeaſes, is ſuch, and ſo frequently aſſailing both the public and individuals ear, that it muſt be quite unneceſſary for me to enter into any proof or demonſtration thereof: to uſe the language of the poet, that diſeaſe is, every day, "making countleſs thou-"ſands mourn."

It is alſo equally well known, that, of all the modes of inſtruction for medical practitioners, there is not one ſo beneficial and impreſſive, as leſſons received out of the unerring book of nature, by the bed-ſide of the ſick: now, I will be bold to ſay, that knowledge ſo acquired, is not more requiſite to the proper and ſucceſsful treatment of any diſeaſe than in the Yellow Fever.

The Yellow Fever, I muſt farther notice, very rarely occurs in England, and then ſeldom or never in the inſidious and violent manner that it does in the Weſt-Indies: it muſt, conſequently, happen, that many naval ſurgeons, and thoſe too, in other reſpects, very able ones, but who have not previouſly ſerved as ſurgeons' mates on the Weſt-India ſtation, on their firſt going to the Weſt-Indies, will not be armed with the acumen neceſſary towards penetrating into the nature of, and properly treating, that very prevailing and rapacious diſeaſe.

THIS evil might be prevented, by preferring and appointing none to be ſurgeons of ſhips of war on the Weſt-India ſtation, but thoſe that had ſerved as ſurgeons' mates, or otherwiſe as medical men, in the Weſt-Indies, and thereby gained a competent knowledge of the Yellow Fever. Perſons, even ſo qualified, might be farther greatly afsisted and improved, by perusing the best of writers on the Yellow Fever, which could be with great propriety pointed out and recommended to them, by the persons appointed to examine naval surgeons.

The learned Dr. Rush, also, Mosely, Chisholm, Brice, and Macleane, have all written, very lately and amply, on the Yellow Fever; but, with all due deference to their opinions, I must express myself to have been so successful, from adhering to the practice recommended by Dr. Clarke, in his Observations on the Diseases of Seamen on long Voyages and into warm Climates; by, also, Dr. John Hunter, in his Observations on the Diseases of the Army in

Jamaica; and their accounts, as well as treatment, of the Yellow Fever are ſo peculiarly well adapted to that diſeaſe, as it appears to me to affect ſeamen on ſhip-board, that I cannot otherwiſe than, in the warmeſt, the moſt heartfelt, and the moſt grateful, manner, recommend thoſe authors in preference to all others: my preſumption, in ſo doing, and ſuppoſing it to be at all neceſſary, will, I hope, be pardoned, in conſideration of the goodneſs of my intentions.

THE benefits of medicine might be ſtill farther imparted to ſeamen in the royal navy, by a greater attention to the qualifications of ſurgeons as to diſeaſes in general, for it muſt be acknowledged, that many, if not the chief part, of the ailments and afflictions of ſeamen in the royal navy, are ſuch as require the aid of a phyſician; in the Weſt-Indies, for inſtance, where a naval ſurgeon finds it neceſſary to amputate once, he will have, I am certain, a thouſand ſeamen to relieve of the Yellow Fever, and I am told that if we except the difference in the diſeaſes, to which ſeamen are liable in different parts of the world, the practice is ſimilar in the Eaſt-Indies.

Hence it becomes indiſpenſably requiſite for a naval ſurgeon to have an extenſive medical, as well as ſurgical and anatomical, education, and, in order to enforce them to it, they ſhould not even be permitted to preſent themſelves for examination, unleſs they can produce proper certificates of having gone through a ſufficient courſe of ſtudies for obtaining a ſuitable education; more eſpecially as the ſituation of naval ſurgeons, at ſea and elſewhere, very often deprives them of the advantages of a conſultation with others.

THE great expence of an education requiſite for naval ſurgeons, the ſacrifice they often make of their youthful days, and of friends and connexions, whereby they might be comfortably and to much greater advantage ſettled on-ſhore; their relinquiſhing the pleaſures and enjoyments of ſociety; alſo, their embarking and continuing, for a great length of time, on the uncomfortable, dreary, and perilous, main, and in climates dreadfully deſtructive to health, in order to ſerve their country during war; and their inability very often afterwards, through advanced age and many other circumſtances, to form friends and connexions and get ſettled in buſineſs; require that they ſhould, and it is hoped that they ever will, be liberally paid and provided for, by the nation to whoſe ſervice they are ſo entirely devoted.

SECTION THE THIRD.

Of increaſing the emoluments of naval ſurgeons on the Weſt-India ſtation, ſo that they may be enabled to provide a ſufficient quantity of the Peruvian Bark, for the relief of the ſick of the Yellow Fever.

WHEN I committed my obſervations to the preſs, reſpecting the inadequateneſs of naval ſurgeons' allowances from government, to the ſupply of a ſufficient quantity of the Peruvian Bark, for the relief of the ſick of the Yellow Fever, I did not know that a regulation to aid them in that reſpect had very lately taken place, by which they now have a very handſome allowance of gratuitious medicines from government: among the number with great pleaſure I ſee is inſerted, the Peruvian Bark; and, as it is very wiſely ordered, the ſurgeons are not reſtricted in the quantity of any medicine, included in ſuch allowance, ſo long as they do not exceed the ſum of money ſtipulated for it to amount to, the benefit of the gratuity is calculated to extend to ſurgeons and ſeamen in all climates and ſtations; and ſurgeons going on the Weſt-India ſtation have now the power of ſupplying themſelves with as much of the Peruvian Bark, in lieu of other leſs uſeful medicines, as they may require; ſo that if they either know, or are made acquainted with, the great quantity of Peruvian Bark requiſite for a ſhip of war, on the Weſt-India ſtation, the loſs of ſeamen, which I have repreſented to have happened through the want thereof, may now be conſidered as obviated: what I have ſtated will ſtill, however, ſerve as a freſh teſtimony how long and greatly ſurgeons and ſeamen have been in want of ſuch aſſiſtance, alſo, how very beneficial it will prove to them and to the country, and ſhew the neceſſity for its being continued, and, perhaps, even increaſed.

GENERAL CONCLUSION.

THUS, as Dr. Swediaur obſerves of the venereal diſeaſe, in proportion as liberal and humane attention is paid to the ailments and neceſſities of thoſe brave protectors, as well as promoters of the wealth, the power, and the glory, of the Britiſh nation; and, likewiſe, as knowledge of the cauſes, the nature, the prevention, and of the proper treatment, of the Yellow Fever is diſſeminated among thoſe who have the direction, command, and care, of ſeamen; ſo will the Yellow Fever, which now deſtroys more than the line of battle of our enemy, abate of its malignancy and devaſtation.

THE ſame liberal-minded writer ſeems to lament and be fearful that this is not the age for ſuch benevolence and philanthropy; I conceive that it is, and do therefore moſt joyfully contribute my mite of information.

F I N I S.

For EU product safety concerns, contact us at Calle de José Abascal, 56–1°, 28003 Madrid, Spain or eugpsr@cambridge.org.

www.ingramcontent.com/pod-product-compliance
Ingram Content Group UK Ltd.
Pitfield, Milton Keynes, MK11 3LW, UK
UKHW010345140625
459647UK00010B/851

* 9 7 8 1 1 0 8 0 2 8 9 7 4 *